Reading
Yellow Pages
for Students and Teachers
Revised Edition

from the Kids' Stuff™ People

Incentive Publications, Inc.
Nashville, Tennessee

Special acknowledgement is accorded to

- *Marjorie Frank for compiling and organizing
  the materials included in this publication*
- *Susan Eaddy for the cover art*
- *Jean K. Signor, Editor*

ISBN 0-86530-557-9
Library of Congress Control Number: 2001094389

1   2   3   4   5   6   7   8   9   10   07   06   05   04

PRINTED IN THE UNITED STATES OF AMERICA
www.incentivepublications.com

Table of Contents

Phonetic Analysis

Structural Analysis

Other Word Features

Word Meaning Aids

Literature, Comprehension, & Assessment Aids

READING SKILLS CHECKLIST

WORD RECOGNITION SKILLS

Phonetic Analysis

_____ Identifies and uses initial, medial, and final consonant sounds

_____ Identifies and uses initial and final consonant blends and clusters

_____ Identifies and uses initial and final consonant digraphs

_____ Identifies and uses short vowel sounds

_____ Identifies and uses long vowel sounds

_____ Recognizes the function of the silent e in making a vowel sound long

_____ Identifies and uses vowel combinations, diphthongs, and digraphs

_____ Uses knowledge of language sounds to pronounce and recognize whole words

_____ Recognizes and creates rhyming words

Structural Analysis

_____ Recognizes and uses prefixes to identify words

_____ Recognizes and uses suffixes to identify words

_____ Recognizes and uses roots to identify words

_____ Recognizes and uses contractions and abbreviations

_____ Discriminates between words that look similar but are pronounced differently

_____ Identifies and reads plural and possessive nouns

_____ Recognizes and understands functions of word endings and letter combinations that can be combined to form or change the sounds and/or meanings of words

Whole Word Recognition

_____ Recognizes a wide variety of words as whole words out of context

_____ Is developing a useful sight vocabulary

_____ Recognizes a wide variety of words as whole words within a context

_____ Uses picture clues to identify words

WORD USAGE SKILLS

Word Meaning

_____ Determines word meaning from context

_____ Determines meaning of phrases from context

_____ Chooses the correct word for the context of a passage

_____ Chooses the correct meaning of a word with multiple meanings for a particular context

_____ Recognizes and uses synonyms and antonyms

_____ Recognizes homonyms; can distinguish among the meanings of homonyms

_____ Uses knowledge of root meanings to determine whole word meaning

_____ Uses knowledge of prefixes to determine word meaning

_____ Uses knowledge of suffixes to determine word meaning

_____ Recognize and show meaning of compound words

_____ Shows understanding of a word's meaning by answering questions about its use

_____ Recognizes meanings and definitions of words

_____ Shows openness and ability to learn new word meanings

_____ Identifies and discriminates between words with similar meanings

_____ Recognizes the history or origin of words

_____ Recognizes meanings of some words borrowed from foreign languages

_____ Uses understanding of word meanings to complete analogies

Word Use & Sensitivity

_____ Associates words with feelings

_____ Forms and describes sensory impressions from words and phrases

_____ Interprets figurative and idiomatic expressions

_____ Interprets sensations and moods suggested by words

_____ Recognizes word relationships

_____ Recognizes and uses descriptive words

_____ Interprets and conveys meanings of a variety of familiar words

_____ Shows evidence that he/she is developing word appreciation

_____ Recognizes the implied meanings of common idioms and other figures of speech

Reading Yellow Pages, Revised Edition

COMPREHENSION SKILLS

Literal Comprehension

_____ Identifies literal main ideas

_____ Identifies details that support an idea or point of view

_____ Chooses an appropriate and effective title for a selection

_____ Gains information from titles, headlines, or captions, and other forms of writing

_____ Determines sequence of events in a passage

_____ Reads to find details and information in a passage

_____ Reads to follow directions

_____ Identifies ideas, words, or sentences that are not relevant to the main idea

_____ Makes use of graphics to gain understanding of a text

Inferential & Evaluative Comprehension

_____ Identifies implied main ideas

_____ Identifies cause-effect relationships

_____ Distinguishes between fact and opinion

_____ Makes generalizations based on material read

_____ Draws logical conclusions from a written text

_____ Uses information and implied ideas from the text to make inferences

_____ Uses information and implied ideas from the text to make predictions

_____ Evaluates ideas, conclusions, or opinions from a text

_____ Determines the author's purpose or bias

_____ Interprets meaning of information found on charts, graphs, and tables

Literature Skills

_____ Identifies plot, setting, and characters of a piece of literature

_____ Identifies other elements of a piece of literature, such as theme and mood

_____ Identifies main and supporting characters

_____ Identifies and analyzes characteristics of characters

_____ Identifies different forms (genres) of literature and recognizes their characteristics

_____ Recognizes effective use of words and phrases to accomplish a purpose in the writing

_____ Identifies literary devices and their effects on the piece:
alliteration, metaphor, rhyme, rhythm, repetition, personification, idioms, hyperbole, imagery, irony, foreshadowing, etc.

READING STUDY SKILLS

Dictionary & Encyclopedia Skills

_____ Recognizes words, names, phrases, and titles in alphabetical order

_____ Uses guide words to locate words in a dictionary

_____ Uses guide words to locate entries in an encyclopedia

_____ Identifies key words for finding information in an encyclopedia

_____ Uses a dictionary to find word meanings

_____ Uses a dictionary to find information about words other than their meanings

_____ Finds information in an encyclopedia entry

Reference and Information Skills

_____ Identifies the different parts of a book and their purposes

_____ Finds and interprets information on a table of contents and in an index

_____ Finds and interprets information from an illustration

_____ Finds and interprets information on a map

_____ Finds and interprets information on a timeline

_____ Finds and interprets information on charts, tables, and graphs

_____ Identifies the uses of different reference materials

_____ Selects the best reference material for an information-gathering task

Library Skills

_____ Shows understanding of the library system for classifying fiction

_____ Shows understanding of the library system for classifying nonfiction

_____ Understands how to use a library catalog to locate books

_____ Finds information in library card or computer catalogs

_____ Shows understanding of categories of books—fiction, biography, and other nonfiction

Study Skills

_____ Takes notes or forms good questions to gain information from a resource

_____ Gains information quickly by skimming a passage

_____ Identifies ideas in a passage that support the main point

_____ Summarizes or paraphrases a passage

_____ Organizes facts to support a conclusion

_____ Uses or makes an outline to gain or display information

_____ Develops increased reading rate, accuracy, and independence

Reading Yellow Pages, Revised Edition

INITIAL CONSONANTS

b	bite	bed	bee	bib	bone	bad	boat	bug
d	duck	desk	dot	dip	date	dump	dial	dirt
f	fan	fire	fist	food	four	foot	friend	feather
h	hay	hat	hit	hen	hill	hand	hook	hammer
j	jar	jump	jelly	jog	June	jet	jacket	jiggle
k	kite	kiss	keep	king	kick	kind	kid	kitchen
l	lamp	lamb	lips	leaf	letter	lucky	lock	listen
m	mash	mop	much	mess	mitten	mustard	moist	mouse
n	nest	nine	night	nap	net	needle	number	noodle
p	pie	pot	pig	party	puppet	pat	pink	picture
qu	queen	quick	quilt	quit	quill	quote	quarter	quiet
r	red	rock	rip	rat	run	riddle	ring	rent
s	sack	six	sock	seven	sister	soap	silly	submarine
t	tent	tooth	tub	ten	toe	table	tummy	teacher
v	vote	visit	van	vat	vest	verse	victory	vegetable
w	wish	waste	wig	water	witch	wash	window	wiggle
y	yes	yarn	yawn	yell	you	yellow	yikes	yesterday
z	zip	zoo	zebra	zoom	zap	zone	zipper	zero

FINAL CONSONANTS

b	bib	tub	crab	web	knob	grab	rib	blob
d	shed	cloud	lizard	sled	mud	sad	liked	flood
f	leaf	shelf	roof	loaf	sniff	half	cuff	goof
g	frog	pig	log	tag	egg	rug	bug	slug
k	hook	sink	fork	kick	park	lack	cook	jack
l	owl	nail	mail	full	yell	spill	snail	smell
m	drum	broom	gum	jam	trim	warm	hem	mom
n	yawn	frown	ten	pin	fan	coin	sun	balloon
p	plop	soap	mop	top	jeep	flop	hiccup	sleep
r	star	stir	flour	color	four	tear	roar	door
s	floss	mess	toss	miss	boss	dress	pass	glass
t	meat	carrot	splat	spot	hat	light	foot	boot
x	box	fox	six	mix	fax	tax	fix	Max
z	buzz	fizz	jazz	fuzz	whiz	quiz	quartz	blitz

VARIANT INITIAL CONSONANT SOUNDS

hard C

cab	can	carnival	coast	comb	cottage
cabbage	canary	carol	coat	come	country
cabin	cancel	carpet	cob	common	coupon
cable	candle	carrot	cobweb	company	court
caboose	candy	carry	cocoa	compass	cover
cactus	cane	cart	code	cone	cow
cage	canoe	carton	coffee	conflict	cozy
cake	canyon	carve	coil	contain	cub
calculate	cape	case	coin	contest	cube
calendar	capital	cat	cold	control	cuff
calf	capsule	catch	collar	cook	culture
calm	capture	caterpillar	collect	copy	curse
calorie	car	caution	colony	cork	custom
came	carbon	cave	color	corn	cut
camel	card	coach	colt	correct	cute
camp	care	coal	column	cost	

soft C

cease	cement	ceremony	cinder	citation	civilization
ceiling	cemetery	certain	cinema	citizen	cycle
celery	center	certificate	cinnamon	citrus	cyclone
cell	centipede	cider	circle	city	cylinder
cellar	central	cigar	circuit	civic	cymbal
cello	ceramics	cigarette	circular	civil	cypress
cellular	cereal	cinch	circus	civilize	cyst

hard G

gab	galore	gas	geyser	golf	guard
gable	galoshes	gasoline	gill	gone	guess
gadget	gamble	gate	girl	good	guest
gage	game	gather	give	goof	guide
gain	gang	gauge	gizzard	goose	guilt
galaxy	garage	gauze	go	gopher	guitar
gale	garden	gave	goal	gorilla	gulf
gall	gargle	gaze	goat	gossip	gull
gallery	garland	gazelle	gobble	government	gum
gallon	garlic	gear	goggles	gown	gun
gallop	garment	get	gold	guarantee	guy

soft G

gel	general	gentle	geometry	ginger	gyp
gelatin	generation	genuine	germ	giraffe	gypsy
gem	generous	geography	gesture	gym	gyrate
gene	genius	geology	giant	gymnasium	gyroscope

Reading Yellow Pages, Revised Edition

INITIAL CONSONANT BLENDS

bl

blab	blatant	blender	blister	bloody	blubber
black	blaze	bless	blithe	bloom	blue
bladder	blazer	blight	bloat	blooper	blueprint
blade	bleach	blimp	blob	blossom	bluff
blame	bleacher	blind	block	blot	blunder
blanch	bleak	blinder	blockade	blotch	blunt
bland	bleary	blindfold	bloke	blotter	blur
blank	bleat	blink	blond	blouse	blurb
blanket	bleed	blintz	blood	blow	blurt
blare	blemish	blip	bloodhound	blown	blush
blast	blend	bliss	bloodshed	blower	bluster

br

brace	brandish	breathe	brigade	broccoli	brought
bracelet	brash	bred	bright	brochure	brow
bracket	brat	breech	brilliant	broil	brown
brad	brave	breed	brim	broiler	brownie
brag	brawl	breeze	brine	broke	browse
braid	brawn	brevity	brink	broken	bruin
Braille	bray	brew	brisk	broker	bruise
brain	brazen	briar	brisket	bronco	brunch
braise	breach	brick	bristle	bronze	brunt
brake	bread	bride	britches	brood	brush
bramble	breadth	bridge	brittle	brook	Brussels
bran	break	bridle	broach	broom	brusque
branch	breakfast	brief	broad	broth	brutal
brand	breath	brig	brocade	brother	brute

cl

clack	clarify	cleanser	client	clobber	clothes
clad	clarinet	clear	cliff	clock	cloud
claim	clarity	cleat	climate	clod	clout
clam	clash	cleave	climax	clog	clove
clamber	clasp	clef	climb	cloister	clover
clammy	class	cleft	clinch	clone	clown
clamor	classic	clemency	cling	clop	club
clamp	classify	clench	clinic	close	cluck
clan	clatter	clergy	clink	closet	clue
clang	clause	clerical	clop	closure	clump
clank	claw	clerk	clipper	clot	clumsy
clap	clay	clever	clique	cloth	cluster
clapper	clean	click	cloak	clothe	clutch

cr

crab	crash	credit	cricket	crocodile	crucify
crack	crate	creed	crier	crocus	crud
crackle	cravat	creek	crime	crone	crude
cracker	crave	creel	crimp	crony	cruel
cradle	craw	creep	crimson	crook	cruet
craft	crayfish	creepy	cringe	crooked	cruise
crafty	crayon	crepe	crinkle	croon	crumb
crag	craze	crept	cripple	crop	crumble
cram	crazy	crescent	crisp	croquet	crumpet
cramp	creak	cress	critic	cross	crumple
cranberry	cream	crest	critical	crouch	crunch
crane	crease	crevasse	criticize	croup	crusade
cranial	create	crevice	critter	crow	crutch
crank	creation	crew	croak	crowd	crux
cranky	creator	crib	crochet	crown	cry
cranny	creature	crick	crock	crucial	crypt

dr

drab	dramatic	dread	drew	drivel	drove
draft	drank	dream	dribble	driver	drown
draftsman	drape	dreamer	dried	drizzle	drowse
drafty	drastic	dreary	drier	droll	drowsy
drag	drat	dredge	drift	dromedary	drudge
dragon	draw	dregs	drill	drone	drug
drain	drawer	drench	drink	drool	druid
drake	drawl	dress	drip	droop	drum
dram	drawn	dresser	dripping	drop	drunk
drama	dray	dressing	drive	drought	dry

fl

flabbergast	flare	fledgling	fling	floral	fluent
flabby	flash	flee	flint	florist	fluff
flag	flask	fleece	flip	floss	fluid
flagrant	flat	fleet	flippant	flounce	fluke
flail	flatten	flesh	flirt	flounder	flume
flair	flatter	flew	flit	flour	flunk
flake	flaunt	flex	float	flourish	fluorescent
flame	flavor	flexible	flock	flout	fluoride
flamingo	flaw	flick	floe	flow	flurry
flammable	flax	flier	flog	flower	flush
flank	flay	flight	flood	flown	flute
flannel	flea	flimsy	floor	fluctuate	flutter
flap	fleck	flinch	flop	flue	flux

fr

fraction	frank	freedom	friction	fritter	frontier
fracture	frankfurter	freeze	Friday	frivolous	frost
fragile	frantic	freezer	fried	frizz	frosty
fragment	fraud	freight	friend	frizzle	froth
fragrance	fraught	French	frigate	frock	frown
fragrant	fray	frenzy	fright	frog	frozen
frail	frazzle	frequent	frigid	frolic	frugal
frame	freak	fresh	frill	from	fruit
franc	freckle	fret	fringe	frond	frustrate
franchise	free	friar	frisk	front	fry

gl

glacial	glance	glee	glimpse	global	glove
glacier	gland	gleeful	glint	globe	glow
glad	glare	glen	glisten	gloom	glucose
glade	glass	glib	glitch	glorious	glue
gladiator	glaze	glide	glitter	glory	glum
gladly	gleam	glider	gloat	gloss	glut
glamour	glean	glimmer	glob	glossary	glutton

gr

grab	grape	gravy	griddle	grit	grand
grace	grapefruit	gray	grief	gritty	granite
gracious	graph	graze	grieve	grizzly	grove
grade	graphic	grease	grill	groan	grovel
gradual	grapple	greasy	grim	grocer	grow
graduate	grasp	great	grime	grog	growl
graduation	grass	greatly	grimy	groggy	grown
graft	grate	greed	grin	groom	growth
grain	grateful	green	grind	groove	grudge
gram	gratify	greet	grinder	grope	gruel
grammar	gratitude	grenade	grip	gross	gruff
granary	grave	grew	gripe	grouch	grumble
grant	gravel	grey	grisly	ground	grumpy
granular	gravity	grid	gristle	group	grunt

pl

place	plank	plateau	plead	plod	plume
placemat	plankton	platform	pleasant	plot	plummet
placement	planner	platinum	please	plow	plump
placid	plant	platoon	pleat	ploy	plunder
plaid	planter	platter	pledge	pluck	plunge
plain	plaque	platypus	plentiful	plug	plunk
plaint	plasma	play	plenty	plum	plural
plan	plaster	player	pliable	plumage	plus
plane	plastic	plaza	pliers	plumb	plush
planet	plate	plea	plight	plumber	ply

pr

practical	predict	price	prison	professor	proof
practice	preen	prick	private	profile	prop
prairie	prefer	prickle	privilege	profit	propel
praise	premise	pride	prize	profound	proper
prance	prepare	priest	probable	profuse	property
prank	present	prim	probably	program	propose
prattle	preserve	prime	probe	progress	prose
prawn	president	primitive	problem	prohibit	protect
pray	press	primp	proceed	project	protest
prayer	pressure	prince	process	promise	proud
preach	prestige	princess	procession	promote	prove
precede	pretend	principal	proclaim	prompt	prow
precious	pretty	print	produce	prone	prowl
precise	preview	prior	profess	prong	prude
predator	prey	prism	profession	pronounce	prune

sch | scr | shr | sk

sch	scr		shr	sk	
schedule	scram	scribble	shred	skate	skimp
scheme	scramble	scribe	shrewd	skeleton	skin
scholar	scrap	scrim	shriek	skeptic	skip
scholarship	scrape	scrimmage	shrink	sketch	skirmish
scholastic	scratch	scrimp	shrill	skewer	skirt
school	scrawl	script	shrimp	ski	skit
schooner	scrawny	scrub	shrine	skid	skull
	scream	scruffy	shrivel	skill	skunk
	screech	scruple	shrub	skim	sky
	screen	scrutiny	shrug		
	screw		shrunk		

sl

slab	slate	sleigh	slim	slogan	slum
slack	slave	sleight	slime	sloop	slumber
slacks	slavery	slender	sling	slop	slump
slain	slaw	slept	slink	slope	slung
slam	slay	sleuth	slip	sloppy	slunk
slander	sleazy	slice	slipper	slosh	slur
slang	sled	slick	slit	slot	slurp
slant	sleek	slicker	slither	sloth	slush
slap	sleep	slid	sliver	slouch	sly
slapstick	sleepy	slide	slob	slow	
slash	sleeve	slight	slobber	slug	

sm

smack · smote
small · smother
smart · smudge
smash · smug
smear · smuggle
smell · smut
smelt · smock
smile · smog
smirch · smoke
smirk · smoky
smite · smolder
smitten · smooth

sn

snail · snipe
snake · snob
snap · snoop
snare · snooze
snarl · snore
snatch · snort
sneak · snout
sneer · snow
sneeze · snub
snicker · snuff
sniff · snuffle
sniffle · snug
snip · snuggle

sp

spa · species · spit
space · specific · spite
spade · speck · splice
span · speckle · split
spangle · sped · spoil
spank · speech · spoke
spare · speed · sponge
spark · spell · spool
sparkle · spend · spoon
sparrow · spent · sport
sparse · spider · spot
spasm · spike · spouse
spat · spill · spout
spatter · spin · spud
spawn · sprinkle · spunk
speak · spine · spur
spear · spire · spurt
special · spirit · spy

spl

splash
splatter
splay
spleen
splendid
splendor
splice
splint
split
splotch
splurge
splutter

spr

sprain
sprang
sprat
sprawl
spray
spread
spree
sprig
spring
sprinkle
spirit
sprint
sprout
spruce
spry

squ

squab
squabble
squad
squall
squalor
squander
square
squash
squat
squaw
squeak
squeal
squeeze
squelch
squib
squid
squint
squire
squirm
squirt

st

stab · static · stint · stupid
stable · status · stir · sturdy
stack · staunch · stitch · sty
stadium · stave · stock · style
staff · stead · stole
stag · steady · stone
stage · steal · stood
stagger · stealth · stop
stagnant · steam · store
staid · steed · stork
stain · steel · storm
stair · steep · story
stake · steeple · stout
stale · steer · stove
stalk · step · stow
stall · sterile · stub
stamp · stern · stubble
stand · stew · stud
staple · stick · student
star · stiff · stuff
stark · stifle · stumble
start · still · stump
starve · stilt · stun
stash · sting · stung
state · stink · stunt

str

straddle	strand	stray	stress	strife	strong
strafe	straggle	streak	stretch	strike	strove
straight	strangle	stream	strew	strip	struck
strain	strap	street	strict	stroke	struggle
strait	straw	strength	stride	stroll	strut

sw

swab	swan	swear	swell	swindle	swish
swag	swap	sweat	swelter	swine	switch
swallow	swarm	sweater	swept	swing	swivel
swam	swat	sweep	swift	swipe	swoop
swamp	sway	sweet	swim	swirl	sworn

tr

trace	tramp	tread	tribute	trivet	trout
track	trample	treason	trick	trivia	truce
tract	trance	treat	trickle	trivial	truck
traction	transfer	treaty	tricky	trod	trudge
tractor	transit	tree	tried	troll	true
trade	transmit	trek	trifle	trolley	truly
tradition	trap	tremble	trigger	trombone	trump
traffic	trapeze	tremor	trillion	troop	trumpet
tragedy	trapper	trench	trim	trooper	trundle
tragic	trash	trend	trio	trophy	trunk
trail	trashy	trespass	trip	tropic	truss
trailer	travel	tress	tripe	tropical	trust
train	traverse	trestle	triple	trot	trusty
trainer	trawl	trial	tripod	trouble	truth
trait	trawler	triangle	trite	trough	try
traitor	tray	tribe	triumph	trounce	tryst

tw

twang	twelfth	twenty	twig	twine	twinkling
tweak	twelve	twice	twilight	twinge	twirl
tweed	twentieth	twiddle	twin	twinkle	twist
tweezers					twitch

FINAL CONSONANT BLENDS

dge

badge	ledge
bridge	lodge
budge	misjudge
dodge	nudge
dredge	pledge
edge	ridge
fledge	sledge
grudge	smudge
hedge	trudge
judge	wedge

ft

adrift	loft
aloft	raft
cleft	rift
craft	shift
daft	soft
draft	swift
drift	theft
gift	thrift
left	tuft
lift	waft

lk

bilk
bulk
elk
hulk
ilk
milk
silk
sulk
walk

mp

blimp	clamp	frump	lump	scrimp	thump
bump	cramp	hump	primp	shrimp	tramp
camp	crimp	jump	pump	slump	trump
chimp	damp	lamp	ramp	stamp	whomp
chump	dump	limp	rump	stump	

nd

and	blond	found	hound	rebound	spend
around	bond	friend	kind	refund	stand
band	bound	frond	land	remind	strand
behind	brand	fund	lend	rend	tend
bend	command	gland	mend	rind	trend
beyond	defend	grand	mind	rotund	unwind
bind	end	grind	mound	round	vend
bland	fend	ground	pond	sand	wand
blend	find	hand	pound	send	wind
blind	fond	hind	rand	sound	wound

nt

absent	event	grant	lint	punt	slant
ant	evident	grunt	mint	quaint	spent
appoint	extent	haunt	mount	rant	sprint
aunt	faint	hint	paint	rent	stint
bent	flaunt	hunt	pant	resent	stunt
blunt	flint	indent	pent	runt	taunt
brunt	footprint	invent	pint	saint	tent
cent	fount	jaunt	plant	scant	tint
chant	front	joint	point	scent	vent
dent	gent	lent	prevent	sent	want
dint	glint	liniment	print	shunt	went

ng

bang	ding	hung	prolong	sling	sung
bing	dong	king	prong	song	swing
bong	fang	long	rang	sprang	tang
bring	fling	lung	rung	spring	tong
clang	gang	pang	sang	sting	wing
cling	gong	ping	sing	strong	wrong
clung	hang	pong	slang	stung	zing

nk

bank	clunk	flank	lank	rink	spunk
blank	crank	flunk	link	sank	stank
blink	dank	frank	mink	shank	stink
bonk	drank	funk	pink	shrank	stunk
brink	drink	hank	plink	shrunk	sunk
bunk	drunk	honk	plunk	sink	swank
chunk	dunk	junk	prank	slink	tank
clank	fink	kink	rank	spank	wink

pt

abrupt	adopt	disrupt	interrupt	prompt	swept
accept	apt	erupt	kept	rapt	wept
adapt	corrupt	except	leapt	sept	wrapt
adept	crept	inept	opt	slept	

sp

asp	crisp	gasp	hasp	rasp	wisp
clasp	cusp	grasp	lisp	wasp	

st

beast	cost	fest	jest	nest	thirst
best	crest	fist	last	past	toast
blast	crust	frost	least	pest	trust
blest	cyst	ghost	lest	post	tryst
boast	disgust	gist	list	priest	vast
breast	dust	grist	lost	quest	vest
bust	east	guest	mast	rest	west
cast	exist	gust	mist	roast	wrist
chest	fast	hoist	most	rust	yeast
coast	feast	host	must	test	zest

Reading Yellow Pages, Revised Edition

CONSONANT DIGRAPHS (Initial, Medial, & Final)

ch (initial)

chafe	chance	chariot	checker	chick	china	chubby
chain	change	charm	cheek	chicken	chip	chuck
chair	channel	charming	cheer	chief	chipmunk	chum
chaise	chant	chase	cheese	child	chirp	chunk
chalk	chap	chat	cherry	chill	chive	church
challenge	chapel	chatter	cherub	chilly	chocolate	churn
chamber	chapter	cheap	chess	chime	choice	
champ	charcoal	cheat	chest	chimney	choke	
champion	charge	check	chew	chin	chop	

kn (initial)

knack
knapsack
knave
knead
knee
kneel
knell
knelt
knew
knickknack
knife
knight
knit
knob
knock
knoll
knot
know
knowledge
known
knuckle

ph (initial)

phalanx
phantom
pharmacist
pharmacy
pharynx
phase
pheasant
phenomenal
philosophy
phlegm
phlox
phobia
phoebe
phoenix
phone
phonics
photograph
phony
phosphate
photo
photograph
phrase
physic
physical
physician
physics
physiology
physique

qu (initial)

quack
quaff
quail
quaint
quake
qualm
quarry
quart
quartz
quay
queen
queer
quench
query
quest
question
quibble
quick
quiet
quill
quilt
quip
quirk
quite
quiver
quiz
quota
quote

sh (initial)

shade
shadow
shake
shall
shallow
shame
shampoo
shape
share
shark
sharp
shave
shed
sheep
sheet
shell
sheriff
shine
ship
shirt
shock
shoe
shoot
shop
short
should
shout
show

th (initial) — as in *than*

than
that
the
thee
their
them
themselves
them
thence
there
these
they
they're
thine
this
those
thou
though
thus
thy

th (initial) — as in *thin*

thank
thatch
thaw
theater
theft
theme
thermal
thick
thief
thigh
thin
think
third
thirst
thirsty
thirty
thistle
thong
thorn
thorough
thought
thousand
thud
thug
thumb
thump
thunder

wh (initial)

whale
wharf
what
wheat
wheel
wheeze
when
whence
where
whether
whey
which
whiff
while
whim
whine
whinny
whip
whir
whirl
whisk
whisker
whisper
whistle
white
whither
whittle
whoa
whopper
why

ph (medial & final)   gh (final)   lk (final)

CONSONANT DIGRAPHS, continued

wr (initial)

wrack	wrath	wreck	wrest	wriggle	wrinkle	write	wrote
wrangle	wreak	wren	wrestle	wright	wrist	writhe	wrought
wrap	wreath	wrench	wretch	wring	writ	wrong	wrung

ph (medial & final)

alphabet	gopher	orphan
autograph	graph	triumph
dolphin	nephew	trophy
elephant	nymph	typhoon

gh (final)

cough	tough
enough	trough
laugh	
rough	

lk (final)

balk	chalk	milk	walk
bilk	elk	silk	
bulk	folk	stalk	
caulk	hulk	sulk	

ch (final)

arch	dispatch	pitch
attach	ditch	preach
batch	drench	punch
beach	each	reach
beech	fetch	scratch
bench	finch	screech
birch	fletch	search
bleach	flinch	sketch
blotch	hatch	snatch
breech	hitch	speech
broach	hutch	starch
brunch	inch	stitch
bunch	itch	stretch
catch	latch	switch
church	lunch	teach
cinch	march	thatch
clench	match	touch
clinch	much	twitch
clutch	munch	watch
coach	notch	which
couch	patch	witch
crunch	peach	wrench
crutch	perch	
detach	pinch	

ck (final)

back	kick	shuck
black	knack	sick
block	knock	slack
brick	lack	smack
buck	lick	smock
check	lock	snack
chick	luck	sock
chuck	mock	speck
clack	neck	stack
click	nick	stick
clock	pack	stock
cluck	peck	struck
crack	pick	stuck
deck	pluck	suck
dock	pock	tack
duck	prick	thick
fleck	puck	tick
flick	quack	track
flock	quick	trick
frock	rack	truck
hack	rock	whack
hick	sack	wick
hock	shack	
jack	shock	

sh (final)

ash	rash
bash	rush
blush	sash
brush	smash
bush	splash
cash	squash
clash	squish
crash	stash
crush	swish
dash	thrash
dish	thresh
fish	
flesh	
fresh	
gash	
gnash	
gush	
hash	
lash	
mash	
mesh	
mush	
plush	
push	

th (final)

aftermath	breath	fifth	hath	moth	quoth	stealth	wealth
bath	broth	filth	health	mouth	seventh	strength	width
beneath	cloth	forth	length	ninth	sheath	teeth	with
birth	death	froth	math	oath	sixth	tenth	wrath
both	depth	growth	month	path	south	truth	wreath

SHORT VOWEL WORDS

Short A Words

add	camp	cramp	glance	lamb	pass	sad	tacks
after	can	crash	glass	lamp	past	sand	tag
ask	cap	dad	grab	land	pat	sang	tan
at	cash	dam	grand	last	plan	scab	task
back	cast	damp	grant	mad	plant	scrap	than
bad	cat	dance	grass	man	quack	slab	that
bag	catch	dash	had	map	rack	slap	track
bat	champ	drab	ham	mask	raft	slat	trap
bath	chance	fact	hand	match	ram	snap	trash
black	clam	fan	handle	nap	ran	span	tramp
bland	clamp	fat	hat	pack	rang	splash	van
brand	clasp	flag	jab	pad	rap	stab	vast
brass	class	flat	jam	pal	rat	stack	wax
cab	crack	gas	lab	pan	sack	tab	yam

Short E Words

beck	center	fed	jelly	neck	rent	spend	wedge
bed	chest	fell	jest	nest	rest	spent	well
beg	crest	fence	jet	net	scent	stress	went
bell	deck	fetch	kept	next	sell	swept	wept
bench	dell	fleck	led	peck	send	ten	west
bend	dense	fled	ledge	peg	sent	tent	wet
bent	dent	flesh	left	pen	shed	test	when
best	desk	fresh	leg	pest	shell	them	wreck
bet	dress	gem	less	pet	shred	then	wrench
bled	dwell	get	let	pledge	sled	vent	yell
bend	edge	hedge	men	press	slept	vest	yelp
bred	egg	help	mend	quell	smell	vet	yes
cell	elbow	hem	mess	quench	sped	web	yet
cent	ever	hen	met	red	spell	wed	zest

Short I Words

bib	fig	hit	list	pinch	sip	thin	whip
bid	fill	in	lit	pit	sit	thing	whistle
bill	film	inch	milk	rib	six	this	whiskers
bin	fish	jig	miss	rid	skill	tickle	wick
brick	fist	kick	mist	rift	slit	tin	will
bridge	fix	kid	mitt	rim	spill	tip	win
chick	grin	king	nick	rip	split	twin	wing
chin	grip	kiss	nil	risk	stick	twist	wit
dig	hid	knit	nip	ship	still	vim	with
dim	hill	lid	pick	shrill	sting	vision	wrist
dip	him	lift	picnic	sick	stitch	which	yip
dish	hint	lint	pig	sift	strip	whiff	zip
fib	his	lip	pin	silk	swim	whim	

Short O Words

block	cop	frost	log	plop	slob
bog	cost	glob	lollipop	plot	slot
bomb	cot	gloss	lop	pocket	smock
bond	cotton	gob	loss	pod	smog
boss	crock	got	lost	pond	snob
bottle	crop	hobble	lot	pop	sob
box	cross	hock	mob	pot	sock
broth	dock	hog	mock	rob	song
chop	dodge	hop	mom	rock	spot
clock	dog	hot	monster	rod	stock
clod	doll	job	mop	rot	stop
clog	dollar	jot	moss	rotten	ton
clop	dot	knob	moth	shock	top
closet	drop	knock	nod	shod	toss
cloth	flop	knot	not	shop	
cob	fog	lock	on	hot	
cog	fond	lodge	ox	slop	
common	fox	loft	plod	slosh	

Short U Words

bluff	cup	glut	jug	must	skull
blunt	custard	grub	jump	mutt	skunk
blush	custody	grudge	just	null	slug
brunch	custom	gruff	jut	numb	slum
buck	customer	grumble	luck	nun	slump
bud	cut	grump	lucky	nut	sprung
buff	drudge	grunt	lug	nuzzle	struck
bug	drug	gull	lull	pluck	stuck
bum	drum	gum	lullaby	plug	stun
bump	duck	gun	lumber	plum	stunt
bun	dug	gush	lump	plus	sun
bunch	dull	gut	lunch	plunge	sung
bundle	dumb	gutter	lung	public	sunk
bunt	dump	hub	much	puff	swung
bus	dusk	huddle	muck	pulp	truck
but	dust	huff	mud	pump	trunk
butter	fluff	hug	muffin	pumpkin	trust
buzz	flung	hull	mug	punch	tub
clump	flush	hum	mull	pup	tuck
clutch	fluster	humble	multiply	rub	ugly
crumb	flutter	hump	mumble	ruffle	umbrella
crunch	fudge	hunch	mummy	rug	uncle
crust	fun	hung	mumps	rum	under
cub	fund	hunt	munch	run	unjust
cuddle	funny	husband	muscle	rung	until
cuff	fuss	husk	mush	rush	up
cull	fuzz	husky	musk	rust	us
cunning	glum	hut	muskrat	rut	

24

LONG VOWEL WORDS

Long A Words (with silent E)

ace	change	glade	mistake	shame
agape	chase	glaze	name	shape
age	crate	grace	nape	shave
ale	crave	grade	pace	skate
amaze	date	grape	page	slate
ape	daze	grate	pave	slave
ate	disgrace	grave	place	snake
babe	drake	graze	plane	space
bake	drape	hale	plate	spade
bale	evade	hate	quake	stage
bane	exchange	haze	race	stake
base	exhale	jade	rage	stale
bathe	face	knave	rake	state
blame	fade	lace	rate	stave
behave	fake	lake	rave	strayed
brace	fame	lame	rebate	take
brake	fate	lane	sage	tale
brave	flake	late	sake	tame
cage	flame	lathe	sale	tape
cake	gage	mace	same	trace
came	gale	made	sane	trade
cane	game	make	save	vale
cape	gate	mane	scrape	vane
case	gave	mate	shade	wade
cave	gaze	maze	shake	wage

Long I Words (with silent E)

abide	fine	mine	shire	tripe
advice	fire	mire	shrine	twice
advise	five	mite	sire	vice
arrive	glide	nice	size	vile
aside	grime	nine	slice	vine
beside	gripe	pile	slime	vise
bide	hive	pine	smile	while
bile	ice	pipe	spice	whine
bite	ire	price	splice	white
bribe	kite	prime	strife	wide
bride	knife	prize	stripe	wife
brine	lice	rice	strive	wine
chide	life	rife	swipe	wipe
chime	lime	rile	thrice	wire
chive	line	ripe	thrive	wise
cite	live	rise	tile	
crime	mice	rite	time	
fife	mile	scribe	tire	
file	mime	shine	tribe	

Long O Words (with silent E)

abode	cope	grope	node	rope	strobe
bode	cove	hole	nose	rose	strode
bone	drone	home	note	rote	stroke
broke	dole	hone	phone	rove	those
choke	dome	hope	poke	scope	throne
chose	dope	hose	pole	slope	tole
chrome	dose	joke	pope	smoke	tone
clone	dote	lobe	pose	smote	tote
close	doze	lone	probe	sole	vote
clothe	drone	lope	prone	stoke	woke
clove	drove	mode	quote	stole	yoke
coke	froze	mole	robe	stone	zone
cone	globe	mope	rode	stove	

Long U Words (with silent E)

brute	dude	fume	nude	ruse
butte	duke	huge	prude	spruce
chute	dune	jute	prune	tube
cube	dupe	mule	pure	tune
cute	flute	mute	rule	Yule

Final Y (producing Long E Sound)

alley	drowsy	grocery	jockey	naughty	stingy
army	easy	happy	journey	navy	study
baby	factory	hardy	jury	nursery	surgery
bunny	fairy	heavy	lady	party	taffy
bury	family	hockey	lazy	penny	tiny
busy	fancy	honey	liberty	plenty	twenty
canary	funny	hungry	lucky	pony	ugly
city	furry	hurry	memory	poppy	very
country	fury	ivory	money	quickly	weary
county	glory	ivy	mystery	rocky	zany

Final Y (producing Long I Sound)

buy	dry	my	sky	spy	why
by	fly	pry	sly	sty	wry
cry	fry	shy	spry	try	

Reading Yellow Pages, Revised Edition

VOWEL DIGRAPHS

ai (long A sound)

aid	chain	faith	laid	pain	rain	strait	wail
aide	chaise	flail	lain	paint	raise	tail	wain
ail	claim	frail	maid	plain	sail	taint	waist
aim	daily	gaily	mail	plait	saint	trail	wait
bail	dainty	gain	main	praise	slain	train	waive
bait	drain	gait	maize	quail	snail	trait	
braid	fail	grain	nail	quaint	staid	twain	
brain	fain	hail	paid	raid	stain	vain	
braise	faint	jail	pail	rail	strain	waif	

ay (long A sound)

astray	bray	dismay	gay	lay	play	slay	stray
away	clay	dray	gray	may	pray	splay	tray
bay	crayon	flay	hay	nay	ray	spray	way
betray	day	fray	jay	pay	say	stay	

ea (long E sound)

beach	cheat	ease	heave	neat	read	steal
bead	clean	east	knead	pea	real	steam
beak	cleat	eat	lead	peace	reap	streak
beam	cleave	feast	leaf	peach	scream	tea
bean	creak	feat	leak	peak	sea	teach
beast	cream	freak	lean	peal	seal	team
beat	crease	gleam	leap	plea	seam	treat
bleach	deal	glean	least	plead	seat	tweak
bleak	dean	grease	leave	please	sneak	veal
bleat	dream	heal	meal	pleat	speak	weak
cease	each	heap	mean	preach	squeak	yeast
cheap	eagle	heat	meat	reach	squeal	zeal

ee (long E sound)

bee	creep	freed	knee	queen	sheep	steeple
beech	deed	freeze	lee	reed	sheet	street
beep	deem	geese	leech	reek	sleet	teem
between	deep	glee	leek	reel	sleeve	teeth
bleed	eel	greed	meek	screech	sneeze	thee
breech	fee	green	meet	screen	speech	three
breed	feed	greet	need	seed	speed	tree
breeze	feel	heed	peek	seek	spleen	tweed
cheek	feet	heel	peel	seem	spree	weed
cheese	flee	jeep	peep	seen	squeeze	weep
creed	fleet	keel	peeve	seep	steel	wheel
creek	free	keen	preen	sheen	steep	wheeze

oa (long O sound)

afloat	float	loaves	roast
bloat	foal	moan	roaster
boast	foam	moat	shoal
boat	gloat	oaf	soak
broach	groan	oak	soap
cloak	groat	oaken	throat
coach	hoax	oat	toad
coal	load	oath	toast
cost	loaf	poach	toaster
coaster	loafer	poacher	whoa
coat	loam	roach	
coax	loan	road	
croak	loathe	roan	

oo (as in boot)

aloof	fool	noose	spoof
bloom	gloom	pool	spool
boom	goo	proof	spoon
boost	goose	roof	stool
booster	groom	room	stoop
boo	hoop	roost	swoop
boot	hoot	rooster	too
brood	loom	root	toot
cool	loose	school	tooth
coop	loot	scoop	troop
doom	moo	shoot	whoop
drool	mood	sloop	zoo
droop	moose	smooth	
food	noon	snooze	

oo (as in book)

book	foot	moor	stood
boor	good	nook	took
brook	hood	poor	wool
cook	hoof	rook	
cookies	hook	shook	
crook	look	soot	

ue (as in blue)

accrue	due	gruel	sue
blue	duel	hue	true
clue	ensue	pursue	
cruel	fuel	rue	
cue	glue	subdue	

Reading Yellow Pages, Revised Edition

DIPHTHONGS

au						
	applause	author	caution	gaunt	laundry	taught
	auction	auto	clause	gauze	laurel	taunt
	audience	autograph	daub	haughty	maul	taut
	audit	autumn	daughter	haul	naughty	vault
	audition	bauble	daunt	haunch	nausea	
	augment	because	exhaust	haunt	pauper	
	August	caulk	fault	jaunt	paunch	
	austere	cause	fraud	launch	pause	
	authentic	caustic	gaudy	launder	sauce	

aw							
	awe	caw	drawl	jaw	pawn	slaw	trawl
	awesome	claw	drawn	law	prawn	spawn	withdraw
	awning	craw	fawn	lawn	raw	sprawl	yawn
	bawl	crawl	flaw	lawyer	saw	squaw	
	brawl	dawn	gnaw	paw	scrawl	straw	
	brawn	draw	hawk	pawl	shawl	thaw	

ew						
	anew	crew	hew	newt	skew	threw
	askew	dew	jewel	pew	slew	view
	blew	drew	knew	renew	spew	yew
	brew	flew	mew	review	stew	
	chew	grew	new	shrew	strew	

oi						
	adjoin	broil	embroil	joist	ointment	soil
	anoint	choice	foil	loin	point	spoil
	appoint	coil	foist	moil	poise	toil
	asteroid	coin	hoist	moist	purloin	turmoil
	avoid	disappoint	join	noise	rejoice	voice
	boil	disjointed	joint	oil	rejoin	void

ow						
	allow	clown	down	growl	plow	scowl
	bow	cow	drown	how	pow	shower
	brow	cower	flower	howl	powder	town
	brown	cowl	fowl	jowl	power	vow
	chow	crowd	frown	now	prowl	wow
	chowder	crown	gown	owl	row	yowl

oy						
	annoy	convoy	deploy	enjoy	loyal	toy
	boy	coy	destroy	gargoyle	ploy	troy
	cloy	decoy	employ	joy	royal	

ou						
	abound	bound	douse	grout	mouth	rebound	sour
	about	bout	flounce	hound	noun	resound	south
	account	cloud	flounder	house	ouch	round	spout
	aground	couch	flour	joust	ounce	route	sprout
	aloud	count	foul	loud	our	scour	stout
	amount	crouch	found	louse	out	scout	thou
	astound	devour	fount	lout	pouch	shout	tout
	blouse	devout	grouch	mound	pound	shroud	trounce
	bough	discount	ground	mount	pout	slouch	trout
	bounce	doubt	grouse	mouse	profound	sound	vouch

WORDS WITH R-CONTROLLED VOWELS

ar

afar	bark	charcoal	garden	mar	radar	start
arc	barn	charge	garment	march	sardine	tar
are	car	charm	guard	mark	scar	tart
arf	card	chart	hard	market	scarf	tsar
ark	cardinal	dark	hark	mart	shark	upstart
arm	carp	darn	harm	par	sharp	yard
art	carpet	dart	harmony	parcel	smart	yarn
bar	cart	depart	harp	parch	spar	
barb	carton	far	jar	pardon	spark	
bard	cartoon	farm	lard	park	star	
bargain	carve	gar	large	part	starch	
barge	char	garb	lark	party	stark	

er

after	germ	mermaid	perfume	perspire	servant	teacher
berth	her	nerve	perhaps	persuade	serve	term
certain	herd	offer	perjury	pert	service	terminal
clerk	hermit	perceive	perk	reverse	silver	termite
cover	jerk	percent	permit	serf	stern	tern
enter	jersey	perch	perplex	serge	summer	terrain
fern	mercury	perfect	persist	sermon	supper	verse
gerbil	mercy	perform	person	serpent	swerve	

ir

affirm	circle	first	mirth	skirt	swirl	whir
birch	circus	flirt	quirk	smirk	third	whirl
bird	dirt	girl	shirk	squirrel	thirst	
birth	fir	girth	shirt	squirt	thirty	
chirp	firm	irk	sir	stir	twirl	

or

abhor	chord	for	horn	orb	shore	storm
abort	chore	ford	horse	porch	short	sword
absorb	consort	forge	ignore	pork	snore	thorn
accord	cord	fork	morn	port	sore	torch
adorn	core	form	nor	record	sort	tore
assort	cork	forth	normal	report	sport	torn
bore	corn	glory	north	score	store	worn
born	distort	gorge	or	scorn	stork	

ur

blur	churn	furnish	nurse	spur	surprise	turn
blurt	curb	furrow	nursery	spurn	surrender	turnip
burden	curd	further	nurture	spurt	surround	turpentine
burglar	curfew	hurdle	purge	surf	survey	turquoise
burlap	curl	hurl	purl	surface	survive	turret
burn	current	hurricane	purple	surge	turban	turtle
burnt	cursive	hurry	purpose	surgeon	turbine	urban
burr	curt	hurt	purr	surmise	turbulent	urchin
burrow	curtain	hurtle	purse	surname	turf	urge
burst	curve	lurch	return	surpass	turkey	urgent
church	fur	lurk	slur	surplus	turmoil	urn

Reading Yellow Pages, Revised Edition

ROOTS

root	meaning	example	root	meaning	example
act	act or do	actor	mut	change	mutate
ami	friend	amiable	noct	night	nocturnal
ann	year	annual	nat	born	native
aqua	water	aquatic	nom	name	nominate
cap	head	captain	oper	work	operator
card	heart	cardiac	pac	peace	pacify
chron	time	chronology	ped	foot	pedal
clam	cry out	exclaim	pel	push	propel
crypt	hidden	cryptic	pend	hang	suspend
cycle	circle, wheel	tricycle	petr	stone	petrify
cir	circle, wheel	circumvent	phon	sound	phonics
cred	believe	credible	pod	foot	podiatry
culp	blame	culprit	pop	people	popular
dic	speak	dictate	port	carry	portage
don	give	donate	posit	place	position
dorm	sleep	dormant	pus	foot	octopus
dom	rule	dominate	radi	ray	radiate
dur	hard	durable	rot	turn	rotate
dyna	power	dynamite	scend	climb	descend
fer	bring, carry	transfer	sci	know	science
fin	end	final	scrip	write	transcript
flam	fire	flammable	sculpt	carve	sculptor
form	shape	format	sect	cut	dissect
fract	break	fracture	sed	sit	sedentary
frag	break	fragment	sol	sun	solar
fug	flee	fugitive	son	sound	sonar
geo	earth	geology	strict	bind	restrict
graph	write	autograph	stat	stand	stationary
grat	pleasing	gratitude	tang	touch	tangible
gyr	whirl	gyrate	tard	slow	tardy
ign	fire	ignite	tele	far	telephone
ject	throw	eject	tempor	time	temporal
labor	work	laboratory	term	end	terminate
lib	book	library	terr	earth	territory
lith	stone	lithograph	therm	heat	thermal
loc	place	locate	tort	twist	torture
lucr	money	lucrative	turb	spin	turbulent
lum	light	luminous	vac	empty	vacate
lun	moon	lunar	vanqu	conquer	vanquish
manu	hand	manufacture	verb	word	verbose
mar	sea	marine	vis	see	visible
morph	sleep	morphine	view	see	review
mort	death	mortal	vict	conquer	victory
mov	move	movement	vid	see	video
mob	move	mobile	vit	life	vitality
mot	move	promote	viv	life	revive
mur	wall	mural	volv	roll	revolve

PREFIXES

prefix	meaning	examples
a–	not	atypical, amoral, atheist
ab–	away, from	abide, abnormal, abode, abound, abrasive
alti–	high	altitude, alto, altar, altimeter
ante–	before	antecedent, anteroom, anterior
anti–	against	antibacterial, antibody, antifreeze, antitoxin, antiwar
auto–	self	autobiography, autoharp, automobile
bi–	two	bicycle, biannual, bimonthly, bipolar, biped, binary
cent–	hundred	century, centimeter, cent
circum–	around	circumnavigate, circumscribe, circumference
co–	together, with	coexist, cooperate, coworker, costar
con–	together, with	concert, contemporary, conspire, connect
contra–	against	contradict, contrary, contrast, contravene
counter–	against	counteract, counterattack, counterculture, counterspy
de–	away, down	depart, degrade, dehumanize, dehumidifier, descend
dec–	ten	decameter, decade, decagon, decagram, decahedron
deci–	tenth	decimal, decimeter, decigram, decibel
di–	two	dissect, diagonal, dialogue, dioxide
dis–	apart from	dislocate, distance, disassociate, disbar
dis–	not, opposite	disallow, disapprove, disobey, disarm, discontinue
equi–	equal	equilateral, equidistant, equivalent, equilibrium
ex–	from	expel, exterminate, exit, exclude, excommunicate
extra–	beyond	extracurricular, extraordinary, extraterrestrial
fore–	in front	forward, forefinger, forefront, foreground, forehead
hyper–	above, over	hypersensitive, hyperactive, hyperbole, hypertension
hypo–	under, below	hypodermic, hypothermia, hypoglycemic
il–	not	illegal, illegible, illiterate, illogical, illicit
im–	not	immature, imperfect, impersonal, impolite, improper
in–	not	inactive, incomplete, inconvenient, independent, indirect
inter–	between, among	interact, interchange, intermix, intersection, interstellar

Reading Yellow Pages, Revised Edition

prefix	meaning	examples
ir–	not	irrational, irregular, irrelevant, irresponsible, irreversible
kilo–	thousand	kilometer, kilogram, kilocycle, kilowatt
micro–	small	microphone, microfilm, microbe, microbiology
mid–	middle	midair, midday, midnight, midpoint, midway, midsummer
mill–	thousandth	millimeter, milliliter, milligram, millisecond
mis–	wrong	misfortune, misname, misspell, misstep, misunderstand
mono–	one	monotone, monologue, monotonous, monolith, monogram
multi–	many	multitude, multiply, multilateral, multimedia, multinational
non–	not	nonsense, nonsmoker, nonviolent, nonvoter, nonmember
over–	over	overactive, overcharge, overdress, overgrown, overspend
para–	beyond, beside	parallel, paramedic, paramilitary, paratrooper
poly–	many	polygraph, polynomial, polygon, polyglot, polysyllabic
post–	after	postdate, postscript, postwar, posthumous, posterior
pre–	before	precaution, preclude, prepare, predict, prefix, prepay
pro–	before, forward	produce, profess, profile, project, pronoun, provoke
quad–	four	quadrilateral, quadruped, quadrangle, quadruplets
re–	again	reclaim, redo, refinish, relive, repaint, replace, rewrite
retro–	backwards	retrograde, retrofit, retrospect, retrofire, retroactive
se–	aside, apart	seclude, segregate, secede, seduce
semi–	half	semicircle, semiconductor, semiconscious, semigloss
sub–	under	submarine, subnormal, subplot, subsoil, substandard
super–	over	supercede, superego, superhighway, supernatural
tele–	far away	telegram, telegraph, telephone, telescope, television
trans–	across	transplant, transpolar, transport, transpose, transfer
tri–	three	triangle, tripod, trilateral, triune, trifocal
ultra–	beyond	ultramodern, ultrasonic, ultraviolet, ultrasound
un–	not	unclear, uneven, unfair, unfit, unlace, unlock, unpack, untie
uni–	one	unicorn, unicycle, uniform, unilateral
with–	against	withhold, withdraw, withstand

SUFFIXES

suffix	meaning	examples
–able	tending to, able to	enjoyable, lovable, payable, perishable, reliable, conquerable, understandable, washable
–age	state of being, place of, result of	anchorage, orphanage, parsonage, personage, shrinkage, wastage
–al	relating to	commercial, electrical, residential, technical, theatrical
–an	belonging to	American, urban, republican, Asian, European
–ance	state of being	allowance, attendance, importance
–ant	one who	immigrant, occupant, assistant, contestant
–ar	one who	beggar, scholar
–ary	one who	missionary, visionary, secretary
–ate	to make	irrigate, saturate, celebrate, educate, hibernate
–cy	state or quality of	lunacy, piracy, literacy, conspiracy
–en	have nature of	ashen, broken, earthen, fallen, golden, swollen, wooden, spoken, woven, sullen
–en	to make or become	blacken, fatten, flatten, lengthen, straighten, widen, whiten, lighten, roughen, enlighten, worsen, loosen
–ence	state of	difference, excellence, independence, residence
–ent	one who	resident, president, superintendent
–ery	place where	bakery, cannery, creamery, nursery
–er	more	faster, fatter, lighter, nicer, shorter, sicker, slower
–er	one who	baker, butcher, preacher, teacher, worker, runner
–est	most	cleanest, deepest, easiest, farthest, skinniest, tightest
–ful	characterized by, full of	awful, beautiful, graceful, helpful, masterful, plentiful, skillful, successful, thankful, wonderful
–fy	make or form into	clarify, glorify, horrify, identify, justify, modify, notify, simplify
–hood	state of, rank	adulthood, boyhood, falsehood, neighborhood, priesthood

Reading Yellow Pages, Revised Edition

suffix	meaning	examples
–ible	like, or capable of being	terrible, audible, sensible, tangible, legible, invisible, permissible, visible, impossible, reversible
–ic	pertaining to, like	angelic, artistic, athletic, classic, dramatic, historic
–ical	pertaining to, like	magical, comical, theatrical, spherical
–ish	having nature of	bluish, childish, clownish, fiendish, foolish, sickish, ticklish
–ism	act or quality of	heroism, idealism, humanism, realism, pessimism
–ist	one who	artist, biologist, humorist, journalist, optimist, pianist
–less	without	friendless, ageless, helpless, hopeless, penniless, priceless, worthless, graceless
–like	resembling	childlike, lifelike, ladylike
–ly	in the manner of	actively, happily, justly, patiently, quietly, rapidly, swiftly
–ment	resulting state, action or process	amazement, commitment, employment, movement, payment, punishment, settlement, treatment
–most	most	aftermost, foremost, innermost, outermost, topmost
–ness	state of being	blindness, gladness, goodness, sickness, wickedness
–or	person who	actor, auditor, creditor, debtor, donor, supervisor
–ous	state or condition, having quality of	courageous, dangerous, humorous, joyous, nervous, prosperous, generous
–ry	state of being	rivalry, revelry, bigotry, finery
–ship	office, profession, art, or skill	championship, fellowship, friendship, hardship, horsemanship, partnership, relationship, sportsmanship
–some	resembling	handsome, burdensome, worrisome, lonesome
–tion, -ion	act, process, state	action, collection, education, election, narration, vacation
–ure	act, process	adventure, composure, enclosure, failure, pleasure

SOME WORDS WITH SILENT LETTERS

ache	edge	knead	muscle	right	weigh
answer	fudge	knee	neigh	scene	whimper
badge	ghastly	kneel	night	scenery	whole
bomb	ghetto	knew	often	scenic	wrap
bridge	ghost	knife	orchid	scepter	wrath
bright	gnarled	knickers	pledge	schedule	wreath
budge	gnash	knight	psalm	scheme	wreck
castle	gnat	knit	psychiatrist	scholar	wren
chalk	gnaw	knob	psychic	school	wrench
chlorine	gnome	knock	pseudonym	schooner	wrestle
cholera	gnu	knoll	pneumonia	science	wriggle
cholesterol	gourmet	knot	pterodactyl	scientist	wring
chord	heir	know	ptomaine	scissors	wrinkle
chorus	heiress	known	raspberries	sledge	wrist
comb	heirloom	lamb	reign	stalk	write
consign	herb	ledge	resign	sword	wrong
cough	herbivore	light	rheumatism	talk	wrote
could	hone	limb	rhinosceros	thyme	wrung
czar	honest	llama	rhombus	tomb	wry
designer	hymn	menorah	rhubarb	trestle	
dough	judge	mistletoe	rhyme	walk	
dumb	knapsack	moisten	rhythm	wedge	

CONTRACTIONS

aren't	are not	I'm	I am	they've	they have
can't	cannot	isn't	is not	wasn't	was not
couldn't	could not	it's	it is	we'd	we would
didn't	did not	I've	I have	we'll	we will
doesn't	does not	let's	let us	we're	we are
don't	do not	mustn't	must not	weren't	were not
hadn't	had not	she'd	she had (would)	what's	what is
hasn't	has not	she'll	she will	where's	where is
haven't	have not	she's	she is	who'd	who would
he'd	he had (would)	shouldn't	should not	who's	who is
he'll	he will	that's	that is	won't	will not
here's	here is	there's	there is	wouldn't	would not
he's	he is	they'd	they would	you'll	you will
I'd	I would	they'll	they will	you're	you are
I'll	I will	they're	they are	you've	you have

Reading Yellow Pages, Revised Edition

COMPOUND WORDS

afterglow
afternoon
airborne
airbrush
aircraft
airdrop
airflow
airfield
airhead
airlift
airline
airplane
airsick
airwaves
alongside
anybody
anyhow
anyone
anyplace
anything
anytime
anyway
anywhere
arrowhead
backache
backbite
backboard
backbone
backdrop
backfire
background
backpack
backroom
backstop
backstroke
backyard
baseball
baseman
basketball
bathrobe
bathroom
bathtub
bedroom
bedtime
beehive
birdbath
birdbrain
birdcage

birdsong
blackbird
blackboard
blackmail
blackout
blacksmith
blacktop
boathouse
boldface
broomstick
buckskin
businessman
butterfly
campfire
campground
candlestick
cannot
catfish
catnip
catwalk
chairman
chalkboard
checkerboard
cheeseburger
classmate
classroom
coastline
coffeepot
commonplace
corncob
cornfield
countryman
countryside
courthouse
courtyard
cowboy
cowgirl
cowpoke
coverup
crackdown
craftsman
crossbow
dashboard
daybreak
daylight
daytime
dishpan
dogface

dogfight
doorbell
doorknob
doorstop
doorway
downgrade
downhill
downstairs
downstream
downtown
driftwood
driveway
drugstore
drumbeat
dugout
earmark
earthwork
earthquake
eggshell
elsewhere
everybody
everyday
everyone
everything
everywhere
eyebrow
eyelid
fairyland
farewell
farmhouse
farmland
fingernail
fingerprint
fireball
firecracker
firelight
fireman
fireplace
fireside
firewood
fireworks
firsthand
fishbowl
fishhook
flagpole
flashlight
floodlight
flowerpot

flytrap
football
footprint
footstep
forget
framework
freshman
furthermore
gingerbread
glowworm
goldfish
gooseberry
grandfather
grandmother
grasshopper
grassland
halfway
hairbrush
hairdo
hairspray
handkerchief
handshake
handstand
handwriting
headdress
headline
headwaters
highchair
highlands
highway
hillside
hilltop
homebody
homeland
homemade
homesick
honeycomb
honeymoon
hookworm
housebroken
housekeeper
hopscotch
horseback
horseman
horseshoe
hourglass
houseboat
household

housewife	nightgown	raincoat	summertime
however	nobody	raindrop	sundown
humpback	nosebleed	rainfall	sunlight
icebound	northeast	rainstorm	sunrise
icebox	northwest	rattlesnake	sunset
indoor	notebook	ringmaster	sunshine
inland	nothing	roadside	textbook
inside	nowhere	rowboat	themselves
intake	oddball	runaway	thereafter
into	offshoot	runway	throughout
jackpot	offshore	sailboat	thunderstorm
jailhouse	offspring	salesman	townspeople
jetliner	onlooker	sandstone	treetop
jigsaw	otherwise	scapegoat	typewriter
junkyard	outboard	scarecrow	undergo
keyhole	outburst	schoolhouse	underground
keystroke	outcome	schoolroom	underline
kickoff	outdated	scrapbook	underlying
landmark	outdoors	seaport	underside
landowner	outfield	seashell	understand
landscape	outfit	seashore	upstream
landslide	outlaw	seaweed	underwater
lifetime	outlook	shipshape	underwear
liftoff	outline	shoreline	underwrite
lighthouse	outright	shortcake	upright
lightweight	outside	shortstop	upstairs
limestone	outweigh	sidewalk	upstream
lockjaw	overall	skyscraper	vineyard
lookout	overcome	snowball	warehouse
longhand	overhead	snowflake	waterfall
lovelorn	overlook	snowman	waterlogged
lovesick	overnight	somebody	waterway
lowdown	paintbrush	someday	weekend
lowlands	pancake	somehow	whatever
madhouse	passport	someone	whenever
mailbox	patchwork	something	whereas
mailman	peppermint	sometime	wherever
mainframe	pillowcase	somewhat	widespread
mainland	placement	somewhere	wildlife
marketplace	pocketbook	southeast	windmill
matchbook	postdate	southwest	withdraw
moonlight	playground	spaceship	withhold
moonstone	policeman	springtime	withstand
moonstruck	popcorn	stagecoach	within
mountainside	proofread	stairway	without
newborn	quarterback	starfish	woodland
newspaper	quicksand	steamboat	worthwhile
nightdress	railroad	storekeeper	yourself
nightfall	railway	suitcase	

SELECTED ABBREVIATIONS

ac	alternating current		Eng.	English
AD	Anno Domini (in the year of our Lord)		EST	Eastern Standard Time
A.M.	ante meridiem, before noon		etc.	et cetera, and so forth
AM	amplitude modulation		F	Fahrenheit
Amer.	America; American		FAQs	frequently asked questions
anon.	anonymous		fig.	figure
apt.	apartment; appointment		fl. oz.	fluid ounce
ASAP	as soon as possible		FM	frequency modulation
assoc.	association		Fr.	Father; Friar; French
asst.	assistant		Fri.	Friday
atty.	attorney		ft.	foot; feet
Ave.	avenue		gal.	gallons
BA	Bachelor of Arts		GIF	graphics file
BC	Before Christ		Gov.	Governor
BCE	before the common era		govt.	government
bibliog.	bibliography		gr.	gram
blvd.	boulevard		grad.	graduate; graduated
bps	bites per second		hdqrs.	headquarters
bur.	bureau		Hon.	Honorable
C	Centigrade; Celsius		ht.	height; heat
CD	compact disc		HTML	HyperText Mark-Up Language
cal.	calories		I., i.	island
cap.	capital		ibid.	ibidem, in the same place
cent.	century		i.e.	that is
ch, chap.	chapter		ill., illus.	illustration
cl	centiliter		in.	inch
cm	centimeter		inc.	incorporated, including
c/o	care of		incog.	incognito unknown
co.	company		int.	interest, international
c.o.d.	cash on delivery; collect on delivery		intro.	introduction
conf.	conference		IOU	I owe you
coop.	cooperative		I.Q.	Intelligence quotient
(c) cop.	copyright		ISP	Internet service provider
corp.	corporation		Jr.	Junior
CPU	central processing unit		K	Kelvin
CST	Central Standard Time		kg	kilogram
DA	District Attorney		kl	kiloliter
dc	direct current		km	kilometer
dept.	department		kn	knot
diag.	diagram		l	liter
dict.	dictionary		lab.	laboratory
dm.	decimeter		lang.	language
doz.	dozen		lat.	latitude
DST	Daylight Savings Time		lb.	pound
DVD	digital video disc		lib.	librarian; library
ed.	edition		lit.	literature
e.g.	for example		Lt., Lieut.	Lieutenant
elem.	elementary		Ltd.	Limited
e-mail	electronic mail		m	meter
enc.	enclosure, encyclopedia		ml	milliliter

MA	Master of Arts		rd.	road
M.D.	Doctor of Medicine		recd.	received
mdse.	merchandise		ref.	reference; refer
meas.	measure		reg.	region; regulation
memo	memorandum		rep.	representative; republic
mfg.	manufacturing		Rev.	Reverend; Revelations
mi.	mile		rev.	review; revise; revolution
min.	minute		R.I.P.	rest in peace
misc.	miscellaneous		rpm	revolutions per minute
mm.	millimeter		R.R.	railroad
Mme	Madame		R.S.V.P	Answer, if you please
mo.	month		Sat.	Saturday
Mon.	Monday		sec.	second
MPG	miles per gallon		secy.	secretary
MPH	miles per hour		sig.	signature
Mr.	Mister		sing.	singular
Mrs.	Missus, Mistress		SOS	international distress signal
Ms.	Miss		sp.	spelling
Msgr.	Monsignor		spec.	specification
MST	Mountain Standard Time		sq.	square
Mt., mt.	Mount, mountain		Sr.	Senior
mun.	municipal		St.	Saint; strait; street
n.	noun; north		subj.	subject
nat., natl.	national		Sun.	Sunday
no.	number		Supt.	Superintendent
O.K.	correct; all right		syn.	synonym
oz.	ounce		t	metric ton
p.	page		tech.	technical; technology
pal.	parliament		temp.	temperature
par.	paragraph; parenthesis		Thurs.	Thursday
pat.	patient		TM	trademark
pd.	paid		treas.	treasurer
Ph.D.	Doctor of Philosophy		Tues.	Tuesday
philos.	philosophy		UN	United Nations
phot., photo	photograph		Univ.	University
pl.	plural; place		URL	Uniform Resource Locator
P.M.	post meridiem (afternoon); postmaster; post mortem		v.	verb
			vet.	veteran; veterinary
P.O.	post office		VIP	Very Important Person
pop.	population		vol.	volume
POW	prisoner of war		VP	Vice President
pp.	pages		vs.	versus; against
ppd.	prepaid		Wed.	Wednesday
Pres.	President		wk.	week
Prof.	Professor		w/o	without
prop.	property		wt.	weight
P.S.	postscript		WWW	world-wide web, Internet
PST	Pacific Standard Time		yd.	yard
pt.	pint		yr.	year
qt.	quart			

A RHYMING GAME

Here's a challenging game that can be used for vocabulary development. Students enjoy playing with words while they sharpen skills of rhyming, using synonyms, exploring word meaning, and using nouns and adjectives.

The object of the game is to find a rhyming pair of words that presents or describes a humorous word picture. The word pair consists of an adjective and a noun. These pairs are sometimes called "Hink Pinks" (one syllable), "Hinkey Pinkeys" (2 syllables), "Hinkety Pinketys" (3 syllables).

To start the game, a teacher or student gives a clue. The clue includes an adjective and a noun in a phrase where one word describes a noun. The students must think of a rhyming pair of words to fit the clue. Here are some examples:

> Question: "What is a HINK PINK for a chubby feline?"
> *Answer: a fat cat*
>
> Question: "What is a HINKY PINKY for a welt on a sibling?"
> *Answer: a sister blister*
>
> Question: "What is a HINKETY PINKETY for an evil preacher?"
> *Answer: a sinister minister*

Sample Pairs	Clues	Sample Pairs	Clues
drab cab	*dreary taxi*	beach speech	*talk at the seashore*
black crack	*dark crevice*	beast feast	*monster's banquet*
glad lad	*happy boy*	cheap sheep	*inexpensive lamb*
frail male	*weak man*	hen pen	*a cage for chickens*
pale whale	*pallid sea mammal*	bent cent	*a crooked penny*
brain strain	*cerebral overwork*	terse verse	*a concise rhyme*
fake snake	*fraudulent reptile*	wet pet	*a damp dog*
chalk talk	*blackboard chat*	pork fork	*a utensil for ham*
chance glance	*lucky glimpse*	cross boss	*an angry employer*
grim hymn	*stern church song*	loud crowd	*a noisy mob*
limp blimp	*dirigible with no air*	preacher bleacher	*grandstand for clergy*
wider spider	*fatter arachnid*	sound hound	*a healthy dog*
bright light	*brilliant illumination*	flower shower	*a rain of posies*
brighter writer	*smarter author*	mouse house	*a dwelling for rodents*
wise prize	*intelligent award*	fudge judge	*a chocolate jurist*
long song	*lengthy tune*	glum chum	*a grumpy friend*
rude dude	*crude guy*	skunk bunk	*bed for 2 polecats*
book crook	*manuscript burglar*	pig wig	*a hog's hairpiece*
harsh marsh	*rough swamp*	funny bunny	*a humorous rabbit*
last blast	*final explosion*	cute newt	*a darling salamander*
fraud abroad	*trickery overseas*	lovin' oven	*a romantic stove*
brave slave	*courageous servant*	broom groom	*a sweeping newlywed*

SELECTED LIST OF SYNONYMS, ANTONYMS, HOMOPHONES

word	synonym	antonym	homophone
above	over	below	—
absent	missing	present	—
abuse	mistreat	protect	—
add	total	subtract	—
adept	proficient	unskilled	—
adore	love	hate	—
advance	proceed	retreat	—
aid	help	hinder	ade, aide
air	atmosphere	earth	heir
aisle	passageway	blockage	ilse
alike	same	different	—
all	everything	none	awl
alter	change	preserve	altar
ancient	old	modern	—
answer	reply	question	—
appear	emerge	disappear	—
arid	dry	wet	—
ate	consumed	starved	eight
attach	fasten	remove	—
baby	infant	adult	—
backward	reversed	forward	—
bad	evil	good	—
bare	naked	clothed	bear
basis	foundation	summit	bases
be	exist	isn't	bee
beat	defeat	win	beet
beautiful	lovely	ugly	—
been	was	wasn't	bin
before	formerly	after	—
begin	smart	end	—
below	beneath	above	—
bend	curve	straighten	—
black	darkness	light	—
blew	gusted	calmed	blue
blunt	dull	sharp	—
bored	discontent	satisfied	board
bow*	submit	refuse	—
bowl	dish	—	bole, boll
brave	courageous	frightened	—
break	shatter	repair	brake
bridal	—	—	bridle
bright	brilliant	dim	—
brink	edge	center	—
bury	inter	unearth	berry
buy	purchase	sell	by, bye
calm	tranquil	excited	—

* homograph

Reading Yellow Pages, Revised Edition

word	synonym	antonym	homophone
canvas	cloth	—	canvass
capital	principal	unimportant	capitol
cereal	porridge	—	serial
chief	leader	follower	—
choose	select	reject	chews
city	metropolis	country	—
clever	smart	dumb	—
close*	shut	open	—
coarse	rough	smooth	course
cold	icy	hot	—
collect	gather	disperse	—
come	arrive	go	—
comic	funny	tragic	—
compliment	praise	criticize	complement
cool	chilly	warm	—
counsel	advise	—	council
creek	brook	—	creak
cry	weep	laugh	—
damage	impair	repair	—
danger	peril	safety	—
dark	unlit	light	—
day	daylight	might	—
dead	deceased	alive	—
dear	beloved	foe	deer
decrease	reduce	increase	—
deep	bottomless	shallow	—
desert*	abandon	retrieve	dessert
despise	hate	adore	—
die	decease	grow	dye
difficult	hard	easy	—
dirty	filthy	clean	—
disperse	distribute	gather	—
distant	far	near	—
dry	arid	wet	—
dull	boring	exciting	—
early	premature	late	—
elusive	evasive	overt	—
eminent	prominent	obscure	—
employ	hire	fire	—
empty	vacant	full	—
end	finish	begin	—
enemy	foe	friend	—
enlarge	expand	reduce	—
even	smooth	bumpy	—
exceed	excel	fail	—
except	barring	including	—
excess	abundant	sparse	—
exit	leave	enter	—

homograph

word	synonym	antonym	homophone
expand	swell	contract	—
export	send	import	—
fail	flop	succeed	—
fair	just	unfair	fare
fall	descend	rise	—
fat	obese	thin	—
feat	deed	—	feet
feeble	weak	strong	—
first	foremost	last	—
fix	repair	break	—
flower	blossom	—	flour
follow	pursue	lead	—
foolish	silly	wise	—
form	shape	shapeless	—
formerly	previously	presently	—
forth	forward	backward	fourth
frighten	terrify	soothe	—
funny	humorous	serious	—
fur	pelt	—	fir
future	approaching	past	—
gain	profit	loss	—
gamble	bet	—	gambol
gather	assemble	disperse	—
gaze	stare	glance	—
generous	unselfish	stingy	—
good	kindness	evil	—
great	large	small	grate
groan	moan	laugh	grown
halt	stop	star	—
hangar	shed	—	hanger
happy	glad	sad	—
hard	rigid	soft	—
hare	rabbit	—	hair
harmless	painless	harmful	—
hate	despise	love	—
heal	cure	infect	heel
healthy	well	ill	—
here	present	there	hear
heroine	victor	loser	—
hinder	obstruct	advance	—
holy	sacred	profane	wholly
hot	heated	cold	—
huge	large	tiny	—
hurl	throw	catch	—
idle	slothful	busy	idol, idyll
ill	sick	will	—
illusive	imaginary	real	—
imaginary	illusory	real	—

* homograph

Reading Yellow Pages, Revised Edition

word	synonym	antonym	homophone
in	inside	outside	inn
inflate	expand	deflate	—
iniquity	wickedness	goodness	—
innocent	faultless	guilty	—
insight	discernment	—	incite
joy	happiness	sadness	—
keen	sharp	blunt	—
knave	rascal	gentleman	nave
knows	understands	is ignorant	nose
late	tardy	early	—
leak	crack	—	leek
leave	depart	return	—
led	guided	followed	*lead
like	same	different	—
live*	exist	die	—
little	small	big	—
lone	one	several	loan
loose	unfastened	tied	—
loud	noisy	quiet	—
low	inferior	superior	lo
made	created	destroyed	maid
male	man	woman	mail
mantle	cloak	—	mantel
medal	award	—	metal, mettle
meet	assemble	adjourn	meat
minor	petty	major	miner
missile	projectile	—	missal
more	additional	less	—
mourning	grief	gladness	morning
muscle	strength	weakness	mussel
narrow	thin	wide	—
native	indigenous	foreign	—
natural	normal	alien	—
neat	orderly	sloppy	—
necessary	obligatory	unnecessary	—
need	require	have	knead
new	contemporary	old	knew, gnu
night	evening	day	—
no	negative	yes	know
noisy	loud	quiet	—
none	nothing	all	nun
open	accessible	closed	—
pain	ache	comfort	pane
pair	twins	single	pare, pear
pale	pallid	rosy	pail
pallet	bedding	—	palette, palate
patience	calmness	impatience	patients
peace	tranquility	upheaval	piece

* homograph

word	synonym	antonym	homophone
pin	fasten	undo	pen*
place	put	remove	plaice
plain	intelligible	confusing	plane
polite	courteous	rude	—
powerful	strong	weak	—
presence	proximity	absence	presents*
prey	quarry	predator	pray
principle	essential	unnecessary	principal
prohibit	forbid	permit	—
project*	protrude	recede	—
push	shove	pull	—
question	query	answer	—
raise	elevate	lower	raze
read*	peruse	—	reed
real	actual	fake	reel
red	florid	pale	read
refuse*	decline	accept	—
reign	rule	obey	rain
remain	stay	leave	—
rich	wealthy	poor	—
right	correct	wrong	wright, rite
ring	peal	—	wring
rode	drove	walked	road
rough	coarse	smooth	ruff
route	course	—	root, rout
rumor	gossip	truth	roomer
sad	unhappy	glad	—
same	identical	different	—
scene	setting	—	seen
scents	odors	—	cents
scream	yell	whisper	—
sea	ocean	—	see
sealing	fastening	unfastening	ceiling
seem	appear	is	seam
sell	vend	purchase	cell
sent	dispatched	returned	cent, scent
serf	slave	master	surf
sheer	thin	opaque	shear
shy	timid	aggressive	—
sight	vision	blindness	site, cite
slow	unhurried	fast	sloe
small	tiny	large	—
smile	grin	frown	—
soar	fly	—	sore
sole	only	several	soul
some	few	many	sum
son	scion	daughter	sun
sour	acerbic	sweet	—

homograph

word	synonym	antonym	homophone
sow*	plant	reap	so, sew
speak	talk	listen	—
stake	peg	—	steak
stare	gaze	glance	stair
start	begin	stop	—
stationary	motionless	movable	stationery
steal	rob	buy	steel
straight	undeviating	curved	strait
stray	deviate	stay	—
strong	powerful	weak	—
stubborn	obstinate	yielding	—
tacks	nails	—	tax
take	remove	return	—
tale	fable	—	tail
tardy	late	punctual	—
taught	instructed	learned	taut
tear*	rip	mend	—
tense	rigid	relaxed	tents
there	thereat	here	their, they're
threw	pitched	caught	through
time	interval	—	thyme
timid	shy	bold	—
to	toward	from	too, two
top	apex	bottom	—
tow	pull	push	toe
troupe	company	—	troop
true	certain	false	blank
unique	original	common	—
usual	normal	rare	—
vacant	empty	full	—
vain	futile	warranted	vein, vane
vice	sin	virtue	—
wait	tarry	rush	weight
want	desire	need	—
waste	squander	conserve	waist
wave	ripple	—	waive
way	manner	—	weigh
weak	feeble	strong	week
wear	don	—	where
well	healthy	ill	—
whoa	stop	go	woe
whole	entire	part	hole
wild	savage	tame	—
wind*	breeze	—	—
won	succeeded	lost	—
wood	lumber	—	would
wry	crooked	straight	rye
you	thou	I	ewe, yew

homograph

WORDS WITH MULTIPLE MEANINGS

act	count	letter	puzzle
alarm	court	lick	quarter
angle	crab	light	raise
arch	crane	line	ram
arms	creek	lock	relish
back	crooked	log	return
ball	date	lumber	rich
bar	deed	man	ride
bat	digest	mark	right
battery	draw	market	ring
beam	drive	mass	rise
beat	dry	mean	room
belt	down	mend	rule
bob	duck	meter	ruler
body	dull	mint	run
bolt	edge	mount	saddle
book	fair	move	sample
bore	fall	mug	saw
bottom	fast	nail	sell
bow	feet	navy	set
bowl	fence	neck	ship
box	fire	note	shower
branch	fish	order	shuttle
break	flatter	out	side
bridge	fly	pack	sling
brief	fork	page	spot
buckle	frame	pass	spring
bulb	frank	pelt	stall
bun	front	pen	storm
camper	fume	pepper	streak
can	game	pick	stroke
cap	glass	pike	swallow
capsule	grave	pirate	tack
catch	green	pit	tackle
cell	ham	pitch	tickle
change	hand	place	tide
charge	head	plant	time
check	heart	play	tock
checker	hero	point	toe
cheer	hold	pool	top
chip	horse	pop	track
chop	hot	post	troop
chord	interest	pound	trundle
chorus	key	power	trunk
coast	knuckle	present	up
color	land	prospect	water
cool	lap	punch	way
corn	last	pupil	web

Reading Yellow Pages, Revised Edition

WORDS THAT CONFUSE

pairs of words whose similar sounds or meanings cause them to be confused with one another

word	meaning	word	meaning
ability	power	**averse**	opposition on the subject's part
capacity	condition	**adverse**	opposition against the subject's will
accede	agree	**avoid**	shun
exceed	surpass	**prevent**	thwart
		avert	turn away
accept	receive		
except	exclude	**between**	use when referring to two persons, places, or things
adapt	adjust	**among**	use when referring to more than two persons, places, or things
adopt	accept		
all ready	completely prepared	**censor**	one who prohibits offensive material
already	previously	**censure**	to criticize
allude	to refer to	**cite**	to bring forward as support or truth
elude	escape	**quote**	to repeat exactly
allusion	reference	**clench**	to grip something tightly, as with hand or teeth
illusion	false perception	**clinch**	to fasten firmly together
delusion	false belief		
annual	occurring yearly	**complement**	something that completes
biannual	occurring twice yearly	**compliment**	an expression of praise
biennial	occurring every 2 years		
perennial	persisting for several years	**confidant**	one to whom secrets are told
		confidante	a female confidant
assure	to set a person's mind at ease	**confident**	assured of success
insure	guarantee life or property against harm	**constant**	unchanging
ensure	to secure from harm	**continual**	repeated regularly
		continuous	action without interruption
astronomy	study of the stars		
astrology	suggestions about the influence of the stars and their positions on human life and activity	**consul**	a country's representative in a foreign country
		council	a deliberative assembly
avenge	to achieve justice	**counsel**	to give advice
revenge	retaliation		

word	meaning	word	meaning
councilor	member of a deliberative body	fatal	causing death
counselor	one who gives advice	fateful	affecting one's destiny
contagious	transmissible by contact	feasible	capable of happening
infectious	capable of causing infection	possible	that can be
credible	plausible	flotsam	wreckage floating from a ship
creditable	deserving commendation	jetsam	rubbish thrown overboard from a ship
credulous	gullible		
deny	contradict	graceful	refers to movement
refute	to give evidence to disprove something	gracious	courteous
repudiate	to reject the validity of	impassable	impossible to traverse
		impassive	devoid of emotion
diagnosis	a description of something that is wrong	imply	to hint or suggest
prognosis	a guess about what will happen in the future	infer	to draw conclusions based on facts
doubtless	presumption of certainty	incredible	unbelievable
undoubtedly	definite certainty	incredulous	skeptical
elegy	a mournful poem	insinuate	to hint covertly
eulogy	a speech honoring a deceased person	intimate	to imply subtly
element	a basic assumption	invoke	to call upon a higher power for assistance
factor	something that contributes to a result	evoke	to elicit
elicit	to call forth	judicial	pertaining to law
illicit	unlawful	judicious	exhibiting sound judgment
emigrate	to leave one's country to live elsewhere	latter	the second of two things mentioned
immigrate	to come into a country that is not one's own	later	subsequently
migrate	seasonal movement	lay	to put or place
		lie	to recline
eminent	prominent	mania	craze
imminent	soon to occur	phobia	fear

50

word	meaning	word	meaning
nauseated	to feel queasy	*regretful*	sorrowful
nauseous	causing queasiness	*regrettable*	something that elicits mental stress
oblige	to feel a debt of gratitude	*reluctant*	unwilling
obligate	under direct compulsion to follow a certain course	*reticent*	refers to a temperament or style that is restrained
official	authorized by a proper authority	*repel*	drive off; cause distaste or aversion
officious	extremely eager to offer help or advice	*repulse*	drive off; reject by means of rudeness
older	refers to persons and things	*respectfully*	showing honor and esteem
elder	refers to only one person	*respectively*	one at a time in order
oral	words spoken by mouth	*restive*	resistant to control
verbal	written or spoken words	*restless*	lacking repose
persecute	to oppress or harass	*sit*	to rest the body with the torso upright
prosecute	to initiate legal or criminal action against	*set*	to put or place something; usually transitive
piteous	pathetic	*specific*	explicitly set forth
pitiable	lamentable	*particular*	not general or universal
pitiful	very inferior or insignificant		
practically	almost	*tasteful*	exhibiting that which is proper or seemly in a social setting
virtually	to all intents	*tasty*	having a pleasing flavor
precipitant	rash, impulsive	*transient*	refers to what literally stays for only a short time
precipitate	to hurl downward	*transitory*	short-lived, impermanent
precipitous	extremely steep		
raise	to move upward; to build	*transparent*	can be seen through
rear	to bring up a child	*translucent*	light passes through, but cannot be seen through
rise	to ascend		
rare	refers to unusual value and quality of which there is a permanent small supply	*turbid*	muddy, dense; in turmoil
scarce	refers to temporary infrequency	*turgid*	swollen, grand, eloquent

SIMILES, PROVERBS, IDIOMS, & PUNS

Similes

She is as quiet as a mouse.

He's as neat as a pin.

The baby is prettier than a picture.

He's like a bull in a china shop.

He is as ugly as a mud fence.

Money was as scarce as hens' teeth.

Who is as happy as a clam?

He's as nutty as a fruitcake.

That is as easy as falling off a log.

When she saw Bigfoot,
she ran like the wind.

She's as mad as a wet hen.

The doctor says I'm as fit as a fiddle.

Try to be as quiet as a mouse.

Proverbs

Don't count your chickens
before they hatch.

A bird in the hand
is worth two in the bush.

Fools rush in where angels fear to tread.

A rolling stone gathers no moss.

A fool and his money are soon parted.

Don't change horses in the middle of the
stream.

Haste makes waste.

Strike while the iron is hot.

A stitch in time saves nine.

A penny saved is a penny earned.

An idle mind is the devil's workshop.

He who hesitates is lost.

When it rains, it pours.

Fish and visitors smell in three days.

Idioms

She bawled her eyes out.

My brother gets in my hair.

He lost his marbles.

The idea rang a bell.

He was burned up.

Go fly a kite.

He almost bit my head off!

She blew her stack.

He's on top of the world.

Will you lend me a hand?

Keep your eye on the ball.

Reading Yellow Pages, Revised Edition

More Idioms

He's not worth a hill of beans.

I think he bit off more than he can chew.

It's raining cats and dogs out there!

He has a trick up his sleeve.

It's as plain as the nose on your face.

I'm in a pretty pickle.

The handwriting was on the wall.

She can really put on the dog.

He's a stool pigeon for the police.

I'm coming, so keep your shirt on.

I'll stay until the bitter end.

He's talking through his hat.

I believe she is full of beans.

I've got to get forty winks.

He has too many irons in the fire.

It was a long row to hoe.

It's not fake; it's the real thing.

You're in the doghouse now!

That is just a drop in the bucket.

More Idioms

That's right down my alley.

He is a pain in the neck.

The rodeo rider bit the dust.

I have a splitting headache.

Put your John Hancock on the paper.

I never see eye to eye with you.

Is she ever in the dumps?

For crying out loud, stop that noise.

I have a bone to pick with you.

She really can chew the fat.

You just hit the nail on the head.

By hook or by crook, I'll get it.

That rings a bell with me.

The judge will throw the book at him.

Don't get your dander up.

It's nothing to shake a stick at.

Hold your horses!

I just had to blow off steam.

Keep a stiff upper lip.

Even More Idioms

He's tied to his mother's apron strings.

She was so nervous that she blew the test.

I was so scared, I was shaking in my boots.

The girl was walking on air after the dance.

I was furious, but I held my tongue.

I'm between the devil and the deep blue sea.

The teacher called him on the carpet.

The storekeeper wanted cash on the barrel.

I broke the window, and I am in hot water now.

He lost his shirt when he bought the company.

After the accident, things were touch and go.

You have to make hay while the sun shines.

Don't make a mountain out of a molehill.

The dead fish smelled to high heaven.

I almost jumped out of my skin.

We played a game to break the ice.

It takes elbow grease to clean the oven.

He cried wolf one too many times.

Don't cry over spilled milk.

He went to ask for a raise, but he got cold feet.

He got into the party by crashing the gate.

He's trying to keep up with the Joneses.

Do you have a skeleton in your closet?

Puns

Did you hear about the smart pole-vaulter who really had the jump on things?

A swimming animal that barks is a dogfish.

"Dash it all!" exclaimed the runner.

The scissor-happy film director shouted, "Cut! Cut!"

"Don't drop the eggs," cracked the grocer.

Did you hear about the snobbish robbery victim who was really stuck up?

If your refrigerator is running, you should try to catch it.

The lawyer concluded, "Just in case."

A kindergarten teacher tries to make little things count.

The grizzly said, "I can't bear these tourists any more."

"I always let things slide," said the trombonist.

The dentist said, "My occupation is very full-filling."

She was very moved by the show about earthquakes.

On his way to the cleaners, the man said he had a pressing engagement.

A teacher without students has no class.

My mom says it's a drain on our budget to hire a plumber.

The baker really got a rise out of that.

The butcher is really a cut above the rest.

"See you around," said the circle.

When the salesman left, he said, "Buy, buy!"

The strangest creature I've ever seen is a spelling bee.

The author said, "Write on!"

A sign hanging on an old boat read, "For Sail".

The tailor said, "Will this outfit suit you, sir?"

A clockmaker always works overtime.

"I want no part of that," said the bald man.

A barber runs a clip joint.

"Hand it over," said the manicurist.

The shoemaker said, "That boot really has sole."

The principal part of a lion is his mane.

The night watchman said, "I've never done an honest day's work!"

Dawn breaks but never falls.

The astronomer said, "Business is looking up."

The Dracula movie was a pain in the neck.

Little demons love devil's food cake.

The seamstress said, "You are sew right!"

The horn isn't broken; it just doesn't give a hoot.

The nuclear scientist left a sign on his door that read, "Gone fission."

The funny surgeon said, "I'll keep you in stitches."

Did you hear about the clergyman who wanted to make a "parson-to-parson" call?

If you stick your head in a washing machine, you'll get brainwashed.

Niagara Falls but never breaks.

Did you hear about the wolf that got trapped in the laundry? At the full moon he
    turns into a wash and wearwolf.

ANALOGIES

An analogy shows a relationships between two sets of words. The words in the first pair must have the same relationship as the words in the second pair. To solve an analogy with a missing word, you must first discover the relationship between the completed pair. There are many different kinds of relationships between words that can be used as the basis for analogies.

Synonyms

Listen is to *hear* as *look* is to *see*.
Quarrel is to *argument* as *rubbish* is to *garbage*.
Sullen is to *glum* as *timid* is to *shy*.
Peril is to *danger* as *hectic* is to *chaotic*.
Noisy is to *clamorous* as *splendid* is to *superb*.
Impeccable is to *faultless* as *mimic* is to *imitate*.
Friend is to *ally* as *enemy* is to *opponent*.
Savory is to *tasty* as *boring* is to *dull*.

Antonyms

Calm is to *stormy* as *boring* is to *exciting*.
Minimize is to *maximize* as *cheap* is to *expensive*.
Freedom is to *slavery* as *initial* is to *final*.
Insolvent is to *rich* as *penniless* is to *flush*.
Down is to *up* as *low* is to *high*.
Top is to *bottom* as *back* is to *front*.
Seasoned is to *veteran* as *inexperienced* is to *novice*.
Big is to *little* as *large* is to *small*.
Few is to *many* as *some* is to *all*.
On is to *off* as *start* is to *stop*.

Categories

Doctor is to *professional* as *miner* is to *laborer*.
Pebble is to *rock* as *minnow* is to *fish*.
Tiger is to *mammal* as *lizard* is to *reptile*.
Spruce is to *evergreen* as *maple* is to *deciduous*.
Hail is to *precipitation* as *hurricane* is to *storm*.
Rigatoni is to *pasta* as *shrimp* is to *seafood*.
Food is to *stomach* as *gasoline* is to *fuel tank*.
Hour is to *day* as *week* is to *month*.
A *page* is to a *book* as a *piece* is to a *puzzle*.

Function and Location

Bake is to cake as broil is to meat.
Bucket is to drip as mitt is to baseball.
Octopus is to ocean as tiger is to jungle.
Sing is to voice as dance is to legs.
Ink is to pen as paint is to brush.
Channel is to TV as station is to radio.
Bus is to driver as ship is to captain.
Bee is to hive as bird is to nest.
Music is to radio as show is to TV.
Siren is to sound as chocolate is to taste.
Writer is to book as illustrator is to picture.
Toe is to foot as finger is to hand.
Nail is to finger as hair is to head.
A ship is to the sea as a plane is to the air.
Cut is to scissors as slice is to knife.
A den is to a fox as a cave is to a bat.
Eye is to see as ear is to hear.
A teacher is to a classroom as a coach is to a gym.
Commercial is to TV as ad is to newspaper.
Ankle is to foot as wrist is to hand.

Other Comparison Relationships

Goose is to gander as cow is to bull.
Yellow is to lemon as green is to celery.
Teacher is to student as coach is to player.
Centimeter is to meter as inch is to yard.
Smoke is to fire as rain is to clouds.
A princess is to a prince as a queen is to a king.
Second is to minute as minute is to hour.
Horizontal is to the ground as vertical is to a tree.
A cavity is to a dentist as a mystery is to a detective.
An insect is to little as a hippopotamus is to big.
Stone is to hard as sand is to soft.
Meow is to a cat as hiss is to a snake.

Word Structure or Word Use Comparisons

Goose is to geese as ox is to oxen.
Skip is to skipping as worry is to worrying.
Bring is to brought as sing is to sang.
Buried is to bury as studied is to study.
Firefly is to campfire as bookworm is to cookbook.
Campout is to outside as lighthouse is to sunlight.
Sister is to blister as sassy is to brassy.
Horse's is to horse as computer's is to computer.
Ladies is to lady as knives is to knife.
Easier is to easiest as bolder is to boldest.
Low is to lowly as leisure is to leisurely.
Neighborhood is to neighbor as statehood is to state.

Reading Yellow Pages, Revised Edition

LITERARY DEVICES

alliteration .... *repeated consonant sounds in a phrase or sentence*

Alliteration usually appears at the beginning of words. It sets a rhythm or mood to sentences or phrases. It is fun and pleasing to the ear.

Ex: Seven slippery snakes slithered silently south.

---

characterization .... *techniques a writer uses to let the reader know about the characters*

This allows readers to know about a character's personality, appearance, motivations, or behaviors.

---

figurative language ... *a way of using language that expands the literal meaning of the words and gives them a new or more interesting twist*

Metaphors, similes, puns, and idioms are examples of figurative language.

---

foreshadowing .... *subtle suggestions within the text or story that give the reader hints about something that may happen later in the story*

This technique increases suspense and leads the reader to anticipate events to come.

---

hyperbole .... *extreme exaggeration used to increase the effect of a statement*

This serves to add humor and imagination to particular types of writing such as tall tales. It also adds emphasis to a point a speaker or writer is trying to make strongly.

Ex: I've asked you a million times to clean your room.

---

imagery .... *details that appeal to the senses*

Imagery makes the experience more real!

Ex: Sweet, slow drops of deep purple juice drip from the corners of my mouth and flow in little blueberry rivers down to my chin.

---

irony .... *a discrepancy between what is said and what is meant or between what appears to be true and what is really true*

It is ironic when a mother, discovering her child has scribbled on the walls of her living room with permanent marker says, "Now, isn't this lovely!" It is also ironic in a story when a happy-go-lucky, friendly clown turns out to be the saddest person in the world.

metaphor .... *a comparison between two things that are not ordinarily alike*

Like other figurative language, metaphors make writing fresh, moving, interesting, humorous, or touching.

Ex: My little brother is like a tornado.
Life is a gift waiting to be opened.
Without you, I'm a leaf tossed in a cyclone.
The toaster attacks my toast with its tongue of fire.

mood .... *the feeling in a piece of writing*

Mood is set by a combination of the words and sounds used, the setting, the imagery, and the details. Mood may give a feeling of mystery, rush, softness, cold, fear, darkness, etc.

onomatopoeia .... *use of a word that makes the same sound as its meaning or a word that sounds like the same sound that an object actually makes*

The use of onomatopoeia adds auditory appeal and makes the writing more interesting.

Ex: The fire crackles and spits, pops and hisses.

parody .... *a work that makes fun of another work by imitating some aspect of the other writer's style*

A parody is often enjoyable to readers because it humorously exaggerates features of the work it is imitating in order to convey a message, launch a critique, or just amuse the reader.

personification .... *giving human characteristics to a nonliving object*

Personification compares two dissimilar things by attributing human thoughts, feelings, appearances, actions, or attitudes to an object or animal.

Ex: The lightning reached down with forked fingers and scratched the ground.
A massive rock bridge gazes up at the cloudless sky.
Whipping wind licks at my chapped face.
The river sings a lazy, bubbling tune to me.

plot .... *a series of events that the writer uses to make a story*

The plot usually contains the telling of a situation or problem, the development of the situation to a peak of action (the climax), and a final resolving of the problem or situation.

point of view .... *lets the reader know who is telling the story*

The story may be told by a character in the story, a narrator who is in the story, or a narrator who is not in the story. Within the story, a character may tell the story about himself or herself (first person) or about others (with or without including herself or himself). Some stories have a series of narrators speaking in first or second person.

rhyme .... *repeating of sounds*

Rhymes may occur at the ends of lines or within the lines.

Ex: There once was a gal from Dubuque
  who was anxious to marry a duke.
Ex: The kite was sliding and gliding, slipping and flipping.

satire .... *writing that makes fun of the shortcoming of people, systems, or institutions for the purpose of enlightening readers and/or bringing about a change*

Satires are often written about governmental systems or persons of power and influence. They can range from light fun-making to harsh, bitter mockery.

setting .... *the place where a story or event occurs*

The setting may be real or imaginary. Setting also includes the time period covered by the story.

simile .... *a comparison between two unlike things, using the word like or as to connect the two*

Like other figures of speech, similes make writing fresh, interesting, moving, humorous, or touching. They surprise and delight the reader and make the description or explanation more real to the reader.

Ex: July moves as slowly as a sleepy snail.
  Life is like a dark pool of water.
  Math problems are like hot, boring days that never end.
  That idea is as empty as my bank account.

theme .... *the main meaning or idea of a piece of writing*

It includes the topic and a viewpoint or opinion about the topic.

tone .... *the approach a writer takes toward a topic*

The tone may be playful, hostile, humorous, serious, argumentative, etc.

SOME GREAT WAYS TO SHARE A BOOK

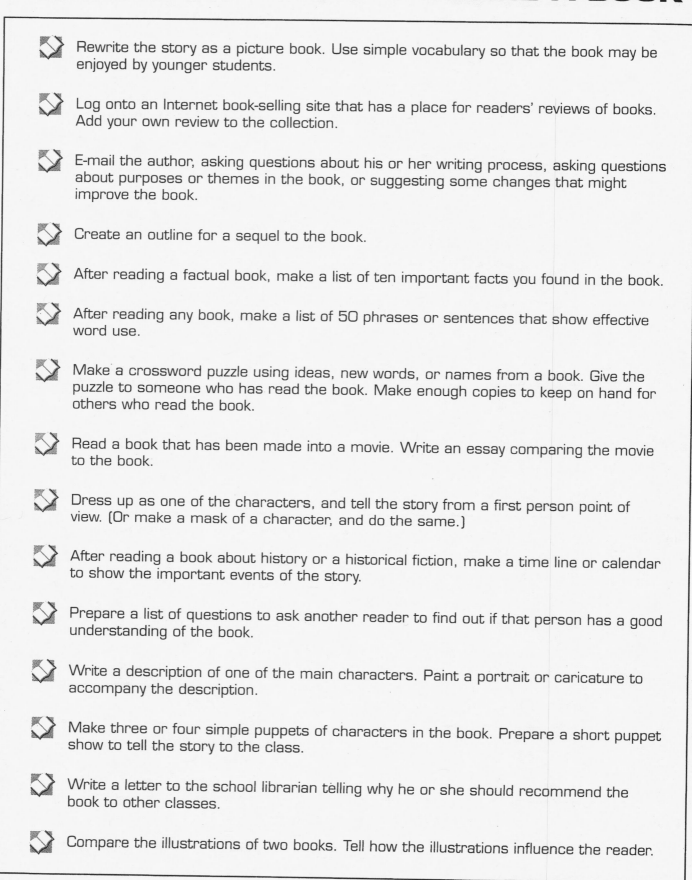

- Rewrite the story as a picture book. Use simple vocabulary so that the book may be enjoyed by younger students.

- Log onto an Internet book-selling site that has a place for readers' reviews of books. Add your own review to the collection.

- E-mail the author, asking questions about his or her writing process, asking questions about purposes or themes in the book, or suggesting some changes that might improve the book.

- Create an outline for a sequel to the book.

- After reading a factual book, make a list of ten important facts you found in the book.

- After reading any book, make a list of 50 phrases or sentences that show effective word use.

- Make a crossword puzzle using ideas, new words, or names from a book. Give the puzzle to someone who has read the book. Make enough copies to keep on hand for others who read the book.

- Read a book that has been made into a movie. Write an essay comparing the movie to the book.

- Dress up as one of the characters, and tell the story from a first person point of view. (Or make a mask of a character, and do the same.)

- After reading a book about history or a historical fiction, make a time line or calendar to show the important events of the story.

- Prepare a list of questions to ask another reader to find out if that person has a good understanding of the book.

- Write a description of one of the main characters. Paint a portrait or caricature to accompany the description.

- Make three or four simple puppets of characters in the book. Prepare a short puppet show to tell the story to the class.

- Write a letter to the school librarian telling why he or she should recommend the book to other classes.

- Compare the illustrations of two books. Tell how the illustrations influence the reader.

Reading Yellow Pages, Revised Edition

- Write a letter recommending the book to a friend or relative in another city.

- Write a book review to be printed in the school newspaper.

- Make a map showing where the story took place.

- Write a diary from the main character's viewpoint to explain the events of the story.

- Make a list of questions you would ask one of the characters in the book if you could interview him or her.

- Create a different beginning, middle, or ending for the story.

- For a non-fiction book, write a list of 10–20 questions or facts that are NOT covered in the book.

- Write a letter to the main character of the book. Ask a question, protest some situation, make a complaint or suggestion, etc.

- Change the story into a feature news article with a headline that tells the story as it might be found on the front page of a newspaper in the town where the story takes place.

- Draw several illustrations to accompany the book. Be prepared to tell the story to the class, using pictures as aids.

- Add a synopsis of the book to your website. Create illustrations to go along with the review.

- Make a travel poster inviting tourists to visit the settings of the book.

- If your book is a poetry book, make a scrapbook containing 15 or 20 of your favorite poems.

- If the book is a poetry book, write at least one poem mimicking the style of the poet.

- After reading a joke and riddle book, make a scrapbook of original jokes and riddles.

- Re-write the story from the point of view of a different character (or an animal or inanimate object in the story).

- Re-write the story as a poem, advertisement, essay, TV script, myth, tall tale, fable, or other form of literature.

- Make a poster, banner, or magazine ad which advertises your book.

- Re-tell your story to an audience without using any spoken or written words.

READING PERFORMANCE ASSESSMENT GUIDE

Have student read a sample orally. Then check the following areas of performance. The performance descriptions given constitute a level of high competency in each area.

ORAL READING PERFORMANCE

Pace
- Pace mostly or always matches a pace of normal conversation.

Flow
- Reading is consistently smooth with few disruptions. Student corrects errors quickly and smoothly.

Phrasing
- The phrasing and breathing are natural.
- The student mostly or consistently uses appropriate-length phrases for conversing, including some long phrases.
- The student includes natural expression within the phrases.

RE-TELLING

Clarity
- The retelling is very clear and organized, showing good understanding of the whole piece and of the correct sequence.

Completeness
- The retelling contains a clear and accurate telling of the main point or idea.
- The retelling includes all the main events, points, or developments.
- The retelling includes important details.
- The retelling covers the story in the correct sequence.

ORAL RESPONSE TO COMPREHENSION QUESTIONS

Main Idea
- When questioned, the student can clearly explain the main idea or ideas.

Details
- The student can identify specific details that support the main idea or that describe characters, setting, or plot development.

Personal Connection
- The student can relate events, situations, or feelings from the piece to his or her own life experiences.

Inference & Evaluation
- The student can make generalizations from text ideas to situations outside of the text.
- The student can make predictions with good text evidence to support them.
- The student can draw conclusions with good text evidence to support them.

Reading Yellow Pages, Revised Edition

WRITTEN RESPONSE TO PASSAGE

Comprehension
- Student's response shows an understanding of the main point(s) or idea(s).
- Student's response shows a clear understanding of the supporting details.
- Student is able to use specific details from the text to support conclusions, interpretations, and opinions.
- Student is able to reach conclusions and form inferences from the text to convey meaning.

Critical Analysis of Text
- Student can identify the author's purpose.
- Student can identify the author's biases and give specific evidence from the text to demonstrate the biases.
- Student can identify specific techniques of style used by the author to convey the message and explain how those techniques are (or are not) effective in accomplishing the author's purpose or conveying the intended message.
- Student uses specific details or evidence to support the inferences, conclusions, and judgments made about the author's style and the effectiveness of the text.

Making Connections
- Student's response makes insightful connections between the ideas or message of the passage to events and circumstances in the world outside of the text.
- Student's response shows that the student has thoughtfully connected the ideas and conclusions of the passage to his or her own life situations.
- Student can relate personal experiences or feelings that are similar to or different from those found in the text.
- Student's response relates the lives, circumstances, or feelings of specific characters in the text to real-life situations.
- Student's response shows that the student has thoughtfully connected the ideas and conclusions of the passage to conclusions and ideas from other written texts.
- Student's response relates the lives, circumstances, or feelings of specific characters in the text to those in other written texts.
- Student's response shows that student understands how personal, cultural, or historical factors in the author's life may have affected the style, opinions, message, or purpose.